Digger

The Story of Charles Sando Karnes in World War II

TERRY CREEKMORE

Publishing Coordinator & Book Designer – Sharon Kizziah-Holmes

Indie Pub Press
Springfield, Missouri

ISBN -13: 978-1-970560-20-6 (Color Paperback)
ISBN -13: 978-1-970560-21-3 (Color Hardback)
ISBN -13: 978-1-970560-22-0 (B & W Paperbacck)

Dedication

For Helen Karnes
(March 19, 1915 - March 23, 2003)

ACKNOWLEDGEMENTS

This dedicatory would be but a hollow shell of a tale without the stories of Gene Greenberg, John Skene, Max Martin, and Jim Hansen; men who fought, and survived, and graciously volunteered to share their life altering experiences. Their oral histories provide a brief glimpse into the maelstrom of World War II for those of us with a family connection to this drama, although none of us can truly understand the dark, visceral, reality lurking behind the words. I hope the families of these heroes are aware of their oral histories and cherish them for the treasures they are.

C.S. KARNES OUTFIT

102nd Infantry Division Made An Excellent Record in War

By THEODORE P. WAGNER
Of the Post-Dispatch Staff

102nd on Parade

Members of the 102nd Reserve Infantry Division, which is scheduled to be disbanded, marching in an Armed Forces day parade in St. Louis.

Louisiana Maneuvers

Key City Captured

Commanded by Sverdrup

Stix, Baer & Fuller

And Johnney came marching home again Harrah! Harrah!

"The nation which forgets its defenders will be itself forgotten."

Calvin Coolidge

"At the core, the American citizen soldiers knew the difference between right and wrong, and they didn't want to live in a world in which wrong prevailed. So they fought, and won, and we all of us, living and yet to be born, must be forever profoundly grateful."

Stephen Ambrose

Digger Karnes, 1944

INTRODUCTION

This project began as an effort to document the experiences of my wife's grandfather, Charles Sando "Digger" Karnes, during his service with the 102nd Ozark Division in Germany during WWII. My intent was to gather all the available information in one place for future family members. Digger died December 19, 1965, long before most people considered collecting the histories of the typical veteran. When I began this endeavor, the only resources available were a box containing a few 60-year-old documents, his medals, and a folded American flag.

However, armed with a new computer, I soon discovered the efforts of those individuals, who with great foresight, have recorded the histories of WWII veterans. The project, *World War II Stories in Their Own Words,* contains a surprising number of oral histories for members of Company F, 405th Regiment, 102nd Infantry Division in which Digger served in combat during 1944 and 1945. Narratives from soldiers such as Gene Greenberg, John Skene, Max Martin, and Jim Hansen provide a window into F Company and the soldiers who are no longer alive to tell their stories.

Digger's early biography is courtesy of Mr. John Karnes and is taken from the Karnes' family history website. The pictures from Digger's photo album have the words, which were written on the back, included as a caption. I also attempted to obtain a copy of Digger's military records from the National Personnel Records Center at the Department of Military Personnel Records in St. Louis, Missouri. The reply I received on February 7, 2007, states," the record needed to answer your inquiry is not in our files. If the record were here on July 12, 1973, it would have been in the area that suffered the most damage in the fire on that date and may have been destroyed. The fire destroyed the major portion of records of Army military personnel for the period 1912 through 1959. "

Lynn Creekmore, Sue and Carl Schumacher, and Susan and Roger Youree provided much needed editorial assistance while Emily and Charles Youree were enlisted as proofreaders for the duration. Susan Youree also scanned Digger's photographs for inclusion in this document. This was truly a family effort.

Editorial Staff
Front- Emily and Charles Youree
Seated- Carl Schumacher, Lynn Creekmore, Susan Youree, Sue Karnes Schumacher
Back- Terry Creekmore, Roger Youree
March 2007

It Begins

Tom Brokaw described them as the greatest generation. Those young Americans who came of age when the headlines were dominated by Tojo, Hitler, and Mussolini. Franklin Roosevelt, in one of this nation's most memorable speeches, spoke of "a day that will live in infamy." Members of the Greatest Generation held the office of President of the United States continuously from 1953 until 1993. World War II veterans who occupied the White House include Dwight Eisenhower, John Kennedy, Lyndon Johnson, Richard Nixon, Gerald Ford, Jimmy Carter, Ronald Reagan, and George H.W. Bush.

On December 7, 1941, the United States was ill-prepared for war. Many soldiers had to train with wooden guns and jeeps dressed up like tanks because the military hardware needed was not available. America's isolationist past was coming back to haunt her. When FDR urged the United States Congress to declare war on Japan, America possessed the world's sixteenth largest military, behind Portugal, Sweden, Switzerland, and Romania. Consequently, in 1941 and 1942 the American military was on the defensive. On January 18, 1943, a ban on sliced bread went into effect in the United States. The ban, aimed at reducing bakeries' demand for metal replacement parts, underscores the dire situation faced by our country.

By 1944, a series of hard-fought victories in places such as Sicily, Midway, and Guadalcanal had turned the tide and America's military industrial complex was producing far more tanks, guns, and airplanes than any other country in the world. The Japanese navy lost four of their six fleet carriers during the battle of Midway on June 4, 1942. In the two years following that battle, Japan was only able to launch six new carriers, while in the same time period the United States added seventeen fleet carriers, ten medium carriers, and eighty-six escort carriers. Along with the buildup in military hardware came a corresponding increase in troop strength. The Greatest Generation enlisted not for two or four years, but for the duration, plus six months.

More than 407,000 U.S. servicemen died during the war, while many more men returned home bearing the physical and emotional scars of World War II, and attempted to get on with their lives. For many months, or in some cases years, those soldiers and sailors fantasized about the day they could return to their hometown and a life of normalcy. When that chance came, most of those veterans tried as best they could to forget the war, and seldom if ever mentioned their war experiences to their families.

A folded flag, a dusty box of papers, and some old black and white photos of amazingly young men is all that remains to remind most families of the experiences and sacrifices of so many years ago. Lynn inherited a box containing an assortment of papers, a Combat Infantryman Badge, and two small black boxes.

The medals belonged to her grandfather Charles Sando "Digger" Karnes. Charles acquired the nickname "Digger" when he was young and digging outside the hotel of John Moses Karnes in Senath, Missouri, and someone remarked, "look at that little dirt digger." The name stuck from then on. His mother was disappointed because she wanted him to be called "Sando", her maiden name.

It was the height of the depression when Digger graduated from high school. He and several friends bought a Chevrolet and drove to Key West and then continued to travel around the eastern United States for a while. Upon his return to Senath, he went into the grocery business. Digger operated the H and K Market for a few years until it folded. A year or so later he started another grocery store, "Diggers Market." At the time, the town of Senath would at best support only one of each type of business, so things rarely had official names, they were just referred to as "the market", "the drug store" or the like.

By April of 1944, Digger was one month shy of 30 years old, had married his sweetheart Helen Marshall, and had a four-year-old daughter Sue Ellen. In 1944, the U.S. military was in dire need of soldiers, but they weren't about to draft a 30-year-old married man with a family, so Digger volunteered for duty. The typical inductee in WWII was 20 years old, but the U.S. was gearing up for the invasion of Europe and was in need of troops to fill the ranks.

One of the papers in "the box," dated April 14, 1944, directed Charles Sando Karnes to report to Local Draft Board 1 at the courthouse in Kennett, MO at 7:00 A.M. on the morning of April

28, 1944, for induction into the army. Another missive dated April 28, 1944, proclaimed Digger to be physically fit and acceptable by the Army for general military service. A third document was an immunization register with dates for a variety of vaccinations including triple typhoid, typhus, tetanus, cholera, and one dated 17 May 1944, for a smallpox vaccination. This vaccination was given on Digger's 30th birthday.

After basic training, Digger was assigned to Company F, 405th Infantry Regiment of the 102nd Infantry Division. The 102nd "Ozark" Division was first organized in 1918 and deactivated following WWI. It was transferred to the Army Reserve and allocated to the states of Missouri and Arkansas. The Division history states, "Since 1921, the Division existed only on paper gathering dust in musty files."

On September 15, 1942, the Division was reactivated at Camp Maxey TX. An excerpt from *102nd thru Germany: WWII Unit History 102nd Infantry Division,* describes the training process required to convert citizens into citizen soldiers.

Time was short, but training was thorough and tough. Recruits, all with sore arms and some with tags still on their new uniforms, streamed into Camp Maxey during October, November and December -- 15,000 of them. On Texas plains where dust and mud abounded side by side, they learned soldiering from the bottom up. They learned to drill, to hike, to shoot, to hit the ground, to dig in, to bracket the enemy with big guns, to read maps, to build bridges and tank traps, to lay wire and mines. They learned to keep guns firing, men healthy, vehicles rolling, rations coming, radios transmitting, and water pure. Pistols, carbines, rifles, tommy-guns, BARs, machine guns, mortars, bazookas, 105s, 155s – they learned them all. They operated as squads, then as sections, and platoons and companies, then as battalions, regiments, and infantry-artillery combat teams. In the CPs clerks discovered the intricacies of army procedure, the "channels", the importance of serving their fellow soldiers.

Those Damn Doggies in F

Men of Co. F., 405th Regiment, 102nd Division [2nd Brigade]

405th Infantry

By July 1, 1944, the Division had relocated to Ft. Dix, New Jersey for what everyone concluded was the final phase of preparation for overseas movement. Since Ft. Dix was on the eastern seaboard, the European Theater was the logical destination. However, the overseas deployment was put on hold August 5th due to the Philadelphia transit strike. The War Department ordered the 405th and 406th Regiments to Philadelphia where the troops soon found themselves serving in the roles of streetcar, subway, and elevated train dispatchers. The transit strike was resolved and on August 11 the men of the 102nd returned to Fort Dix to resume preparations for movement overseas.

175b. Camp Kilmer, New Jersey (USA)

On September 3, the 102nd Division boarded trains for the 3-hour ride to the Camp Kilmer Staging Area. The Division history describes the issue of new equipment, additional training, and a physical examination all within 48 hours. The physical involved entering a large barn-like structure, which was divided into a maze of compartments and stations. Once inside the door, the soldiers undressed then started rapidly walking from one medical inspector to another, invariably to be waved on without stopping. The popular conclusion drawn from this experience was that any man who succeeded in finding his way through the labyrinth and again found his starting point was automatically declared fit for overseas duty.

64. Stacked up aboard ship. (USN)

On 12 September, the troops of the 102nd boarded six ships: the *John Ericesson, Marine Wolf, Santa Paula, Sea Tiger, Bienville* and the *Marina.* The ships carrying the Ozark Division were part of a 74-ship convoy bound for France, and the voyage across the Atlantic lasted twelve days. No record is available regarding which ship carried Digger to Europe. However, Gene Greenberg, who was in Digger's Company, sailed on the *John Erickson*. The two-stack John Ericsson had begun service as the Swedish liner Kungsholm, but following its metamorphosis to a troop transport ship, the accommodations onboard were anything but luxurious.

Gene Greenberg was a Sgt. from New York who served in Co. F, 405th along with Digger. Greenberg's story is unusual because it was documented in a daily diary while in combat conditions. The introduction for Sgt. Greenberg in *World War II Stories in Their Own Words* notes the keeping of such a diary under those conditions was "strongly advised against."

Gene Greenberg served in the same Company as Digger, and excerpts of Greenberg's diary, and recollections from other members of the 405th, are included to provide an indication of what F Company, and Digger, experienced during their time in Europe. While the stories of fellow F Company soldiers John Skene, Max Martin, and Jim Hansen provide details about the high and low points of the unit, it is Gene Greenberg's diary entries that are repeatedly quoted to provide the day-to-day narrative for the men of F Company 405th.

The Battle of the Atlantic was the longest continuous military campaign of WWII. Early shipping losses during what the German Kriegsmarine referred to as "The Happy Times," were catastrophic. More than 270 Allied ships were sunk between June 1940 and February 1941. But by September 1944, the great German surface raiders *Bismark, Admiral Graff Spee, Scharnhorst* and *Gneisenau* were eliminated, and the vaunted U-boat threat was largely neutralized. In August 1944, just three weeks prior to Digger's sailing, Admiral Dönitz ordered the official withdrawal of most of the German submarines from the Atlantic region of operations.

The hard-won victory in the Battle of the Atlantic blasted open the gates for the flood of troops and material which would eventually drive the Third Reich from occupied Europe. Digger, and the other men of F Company, 405th Regiment of the 102nd Ozark Division were the reinforcements for those divisions that had survived the Allied invasion of Europe at Normandy, and fought through the hedgerows of France, and were driving the Nazis from Belgium and Netherlands. The following entries describe leaving Staten Island for France, and the beginning of their great campaign.

Gene Greenberg

Greenberg 405-F

Saturday, September 11, 1944

We left Camp Kilmer with all our belongings and marched down to the train. After the usual delays, the train started and in about an hour we were in Hoboken. The people in the houses along the tracks knew where we were going and waved us goodbye. It was dark when we detrained and boarded a ferryboat that took us down the bay to Staten Island. The lights of Manhattan disappeared as did the few lights of the Statue of Liberty and I knew it would be some time before I saw those sights again. None of us spoke very much and when we did it was a masquerade to cover up our emotions. A band played for us as we waited to board the ship. Red Cross women gave us coffee, donuts, and candy. We were checked off, boarded the ship, and were assigned to our bunks. Went to sleep.

John Skene, 405-F

The big adventure seemed to start with a last fling in New York. We had already been alerted that this would be the final passes that we would receive, and that we would be confined to Camp Kilmer until we sailed for overseas. I recall a fast -- moving evening, starting out in Greenwich Village, getting sick on the subway, flagging down the last bus back to Camp Kilmer, and finding someone asleep in my bunk when I got there, with only a couple of hours until it was time to get up and go on K.P. The next day was a long one, and I would not recommend such a celebration just before you are to leave on an extended trip aboard ship.

Greenberg 405-F

Sunday, September 12.

Woke up, dressed, and looked around. The ship had weighed anchor at 4 A.M. and land was no longer in sight. It was a grey day and the sea was rough. The ship was larger than I thought it was. It was the "John Erickson" sister ship of the "Gripsholen", a 28,000 tonner and the largest ship in the convoy. It must have been a German ship as we found places where swastikas had been erased and many of the signs were still in German. It was the largest ship and the flagship of the convoy. The convoy consisted of 59 ships and an escort of 15 warships - the largest a destroyer. Obviously, there was little fear of U-boats or surface raiders.

John Skene, 405-F

We sailed on approximately Sept. 12, 1944, on the John Erickson, which was the sister ship of the Swedish ship Ripshome. The ship weighed anchor at night, and we woke the next morning to find ourselves in a large convoy, which seemed to grow as the day went on. The trip was broken up by bridge games, shipboard orientation, evacuation drills, K.P., and other varied assignments. I remember our submarine scare -- destroyers raced around the perimeter and through the convoy, laying smoke and dropping depth charges. The exploding depth charges sounded quite ominous, as you sat on a bunk, below decks, and waited for any instructions or commands to be issued. We had been briefed in indoctrinations to remain put, with exceptional emphasis placed on keeping silent. Presumably, this helped our destroyers locate the attacking submarines and/or made it more difficult for the enemy to single out troop ships while he was submerged. We never did find out just what the scare was all about, or if any ships were damaged, or if a German submarine was actually encountered.

Greenberg 405-F
Monday, September 13.

The day was pretty rough (the sea) and many of the men were seasick. I felt funny but did not get sick. We got up at 8 and stood in line to get chow and then ate chow standing up in a very hot atmosphere. It took a long time to eat and doing this three times per day made the day quite short. Lunch was very short consisting of coffee or soup plus a few crackers. To supplement this food we would buy from the P.X. whole boxes of candy that we would devour.

At night I went up on deck and saw a beautiful sight. There were no lights on any of the ships that I could see clearly in the moonlight - they looked like ghosts. The water sparkled like diamonds because of fluorescent plants.

The Division history mentions, "for the purpose of equalizing the work and helping pass time, almost everyone was assigned a daily task." The officers took turns in the holds, in the mess, and at calisthenics. The enlisted men policed the holds and the decks, performed calisthenics, and in one case, painted the interior of the ship. September 14 through 19 were described by Gene Greenberg as routine and boring. But September 20 proved a little more exciting.

Greenberg, 405-F
Monday, September 20.

The sky was grey and a bit foggy. We were in the U-boat area and the escorts were on thin toes. At one time an escort charged a little to our right and dropped depth charges. However it was only a false alarm. However during those few minutes the convoy did all kinds of contortions and maneuvers in order to get ready for trouble. The crew rushed to their posts and in a few seconds had the guns and ack-ack ready for action. These Merchant Marine boys know their stuff and seem to lead a pretty good life.

Every day the gun crew would go through maneuvers practicing for probable combat with Jerry Planes. The ack-ack guns were fired at imaginary planes.

The convoy arrived at Weymouth, England on September 22, but the troops were not allowed to leave the ship. No training in England, no fraternizing with the local ladies, no warm beer, the 102nd was headed for the continent, and for combat. The following morning at daybreak, the convoy sailed for Cherbourg, France and arrived at noon. Max Martin with Company C of the 405th describes the Regiments arrival in France on September 23, 1944.

A Snapshot of My Time With the 102nd

Max Martin, 405-C

Cherbourg, France

We unload from the boat out in the harbor onto metal barges. It is raining cats and dogs. We truck inland into the fields of Normandy with its hedgerows. Four men to a pup tent. It rains nearly every day we are here (about a month.) To avoid the wet, first down is the raincoat, then the overcoat, then whatever clothing we had in our duffel bags. Still the dampness came through. The cool, damp weather makes for a healthy appetite. One morning I ate 15 pancakes. Today, one is enough. Four candy bars and one carton of cigarettes is our weekly PX ration.

According to the Division history, "sunny France" proved to be a country of fog, rain, low clouds and mud. The troops were trucked from the war-damaged pier built to accommodate the luxury liner *Normandy,* through the narrow, crooked, battered streets to an assembly area about nine miles east of the city. Gene Greenberg's diary entry provides a further description of the arrival at Cherbourg by those men in Company F.

Greenberg, 405-F
Thursday, September 23.
We left England for France at daybreak and arrived in Cherbourg at noon. The port took a terrific pounding before we arrived. We did not get off the ship till night. The port was brilliantly lit as there was little fear for German aircraft. We went ashore in barges as the piers were damaged too badly. It was raining now and we waited on the pier that the Normandy once used. The trucks finally arrived and we passed thru the station that was partially destroyed. The trucks took us in a driving rain 10 miles from Cherbourg. We detrucked and carrying all we owned including full duffle bag we marched 3-1/2 miles up and down hill to our area. This is one of the most trying marches I ever had to partake in. When we arrived we pitched tents in a downpour in total darkness. It was 4 A.M. when I crawled into my tent all wet. This was Army life at its best. The area we were in was called Area M-119 and it was to be our home for a month. Quite a muddy home, at that.

Greenberg describes the French locals as not too friendly, and they seemed to never have taken a bath in their lives. The men from Company F traded the locals chocolate, gum, and cigarettes for eggs, and potatoes. Training began on September 27 and continued until October 19.

Greenberg 405-F
Thursday, October 14.

Training. We were shown demonstrations using Jerry weapons and soldiers dressed as German soldiers. Very interesting to learn how a Jerry squad operates. Also saw a demonstration explaining the various uniforms and insignias of the German Army and Air Force. We were given a lecture on security especially with mail that we always have on us. We learned and executed later on line when receiving a letter always to destroy the address, so in case of capture by the enemy our outfit could not be found out. We spent a great deal of our time cleaning our weapons as the damp air in Normandy made them quite rusty.

Greenberg 405-F
Wednesday, October 20.

No training today. Told to get our equipment ready as we would be moving the next day -- not to Paris -- but up on line, or near it anyway.

Since there were no radios we became dependent on two publications to inform us with what was going on in the world. They were the "Stars and Stripes" and "Yank". The "Stars and Stripes" was the newspaper that we usually received two or three days late but that didn't bother us as we enjoyed reading it. "Yank" magazine gave us very interesting articles and last but not least "Sad Sack" was in it.

During this period, new units of the Ninth Army, to which the 102nd was assigned, were training for combat, but supplies of fuel, ammunition, and food were insufficient to handle the great demands of the front-line troops already engaged in battle. To alleviate this situation, the 95th Division had previously organized fifteen provisional truck companies to provide high-speed truck service between Cherbourg and the front-line supply dumps. This supply line was named the Red Ball Express, and it was instrumental in the battle for Northern Germany. Truck convoys traveled at high speed along narrow, winding and often damaged roads, which were limited to one-way traffic. On October 7, the first Ozark Provisional Truck Battalion of five companies relieved similar units of the 95th Division. By October 10, an additional six companies were in operation.

The 102nd Provisional Truck Group shuttled supplies to the front for over two weeks. A typical run on the Red Ball Express began at 0830 in the morning. Twenty loaded trucks with twenty-four drivers, and a lieutenant in a jeep, started north from Bayeux, France toward Brussels, Belgium. Driving with a short break every two hours brought the convoy to the midway point at Le Thillers just before dark. The vehicles were serviced in an assembly line service installation, and the unit was back on the road. The convoy usually arrived at a checkpoint in Belgium about 0200 hours where the drivers were given a cup of coffee and a short rest. Soon thereafter, the convoy was back on the road and the depot just south of Brussels was reached at about 0600. Belgian civilians quickly unloaded the trucks, and the convoy drove about an hour to a rest station where the drivers were given a hot breakfast and four hours sleep. The return trip to France was accomplished by nightfall. On October 23, all officers and men were relieved from convoy duty and ordered to rejoin their units.

John Skene, 405-F

Another diversion that some of us experienced was assignment for the Red Ball Express. That included trucking supplies, ammunition, and such to the front lines. And those people assigned served usually as truck drivers, and/or as guards for the supplies that were trucked to the front combat areas. Some of our people came back with interesting adventure stories about the Red Ball Express duty.

The 405th Regiment loaded into boxcars, and after passing through Versailles and Champaign, arrived in northern Belgium. Max Martin's description of the transportation arrangements leaves little doubt the trip was an uncomfortable one.

Max Martin, 405-C
October, 1944

We entrain at Valognes into 40 and 8s (40 men or 8 horses), small French style boxcars. Our M1s, duffle bags, gas masks, etc. go on the floor and 39 GIs pile on top. At night there is not enough room for all to lie down, so about 8 or 10 men stand in the open doorway. T/Sgt Campbell (KIA) shines a flashlight in the dark boxcar, and when one man turns on his side, he directs one of the standees to the hole. Before morning all have found a spot to lie down. We are on the train for three days shunting from one track or siding to another due to American bombing effort to disrupt the transportation system prior to D-day. We detrain at Charleroi, Belgium. Many of the men have the GI's.

Jim Hansen, 405-F

On the 20th of October, 1944 I walked, crawled, marched and swam the 14 miles thru a severe rainstorm to Valognes, France. There we were loaded into the 40 and 8s box cars for a journey to Tongres, Belgium. The trip produced these memories.

We could walk about as fast as the train moved. When body functions called, we would walk on the top of the train to the engine, drop off, and attend to the needs of the minute, and catch the train as it went on up the track, as the caboose came by. Bathing was rather simple. Just climb on top of the cars when it was raining, strip off, and lather up. It made no difference if we went through a town while bathing. The French and for that matter all of Europe was not amazed at the sight of a naked body as most Americans are.

After assuming the 40 and 8 crouch for 3 days, we unloaded at Tongres and then loaded on trucks and rode to an area inside Germany, near Waurbach. On the afternoon of the 23rd, Capt.

Peterson assembled our company for a little pep -- talk to reassure us. Everyone kept the 5-yard interval as we had been taught in the States for about 2 years. I recall feeling an empty feeling of sorts. It was a combination of fear, anxiety, and about 14 other emotions. About 1/2 way thru the briefing a lone German plane came over and dropped some bombs, it was the first we had ever heard. Confusion ran amuck. I had selected a place to sit that was near a small depression in the ground. When I heard the bomb, I just rolled over into the depression, all the time thinking I was generous for choosing that spot. All of a sudden, I was crushed by a mass of other bodies flying in on top of me. The topmost one was a good 4 feet above ground level. Back to the bomb, I think it lit about 2 miles from the ditch I was in, in the bottom. As sanity returned to us, the company of people crawled out of the garbage pit, the latrine, and other places dug for such purposes. Everyone felt quite foolish.

Gene Greenberg describes the same dog pile in his October 25th narrative.

Greenberg, 405-F
Sunday, October 24.

Again, we had little chance to sleep as we were packed like sardines. We stopped at Liege for awhile and finally arrived at Tongeren where we detrained. We heard but did not see some V-1's near Liege. We spent the night in Tongeren and heard that we would immediately go up front. However, we spent the night sleeping in the railroad station. From the time we went up on line till we crossed the Roer River our Division was the farthest north of any American Division. We were the left boundary of the whole American Army. On our left were the British and on the right was the 84th and 29th divisions.

Greenberg 405-F
Monday, October 25.

Took off in morning for forward positions. We arrived there and were now 10 miles from the front lines. We could hear artillery occasionally. Did not feel too brave now. The captain brought us together and told us that we were actually in Germany and the only Army that was. We were to work together with the 2nd Arm'd division. While he was talking a German plane buzzed nearby and dropped a bomb five miles away. A moment later I found myself at the bottom of a foxhole with the captain and the rest of the company on top of me. With the scare over we dug foxholes, pitched tents, and surprisingly fell asleep while artillery positions near us banged away.

102nd thru Germany: WWII History 102nd Infantry Division

Our turn had finally arrived. After months of training, months of waiting, more months of sweating it out, the 405th Infantry entrained from the battle-soured Norman town of Valognes, bound for the Siegfried Line. The first train pulled out at exactly 210810A October. Five days later the weary, dirty, disgruntled troops emerged from baggage-laden cars only to face a long truck ride to Waubach in Germany proper. That helped a little, and morale took a turn for the better when the destination became known. Perhaps they'd get a chance at the Krauts after all, a chance that sometimes looked mighty slim back there on the dusty ranges of Camp Swift. As a matter of fact they were much closer to battle than they realized, for the following day the 405th Infantry, temporarily attached to the 2d Armored Division, relieved the 41st Armored Infantry, thus becoming the first Ozark unit to see action.

Greenberg 405-F

Tuesday, October 26.

Spent the day getting ready to move up to the lines that night. Were told to take essentials and leave everything else in duffle bags. Did this and carried only a full field pack with ammunition and grenades. This was the last I was to see of my belongings as the duffle bags were taken to a cave back in Holland and were looted of all valuables. When darkness fell we prepared to move. Were scared out of our wits by some American artillery units that opened up a few hundred yards from us. This was our first encounter of war noises and most of us did not take to it naturally. We waited hour after hour and finally about 2300 hours the trucks arrived. We started moving up.

The 102nd Division entered combat in increments. The 405th Regiment, in which Digger served, was attached to the 2nd Armored Division from 26 October until 3 November. On October 26, the 405th relieved the 41st Armored Infantry Battalion in the Waurichen-Frelenberg sector of Germany. In relieving the 41st, the 405th Infantry Battalion became the first unit of the Ozark Division to engage the enemy. The Regiment fought at Beeck then was reunited with the remainder of the 102nd, which entered the line from the Wurm River to Waurichen on 3 November. Sgt. Greenberg describes the tribulations of green troops as they tried to adapt to the vulgarities of combat.

Greenberg, 405-F
Wednesday, October 27*.*

The trucks moved slowly without lights in the inky darkness. We detrucked as it started to rain. We noticed we were in a little town. We moved over to the side of the buildings and waited for three hours. Occasionally some of our shells would pass over our heads on their way to the Heinies. The name of the town was Frelenberg. We were told to drop our packs and personal articles in the middle of the street in the rain and make up a combat pack. We did this and moved off picking up a shovel on the way. The captain took us up front and showed us just where we should dig our foxhole. They were to be our main foxholes and we spent most of the night digging them. Each hole was about 30 yards from each other. A captured German pillbox was bout 80 yards behind us. We made many mistakes and wasted time that we could have used for rest but it was only through experience that we learned to correct these mistakes.

102nd thru Germany: WWII History 102nd Infantry Division

Meanwhile on 27 October 1st/Sgt Cecil Reynolds had been wounded in action, thus acquiring the dubious distinction (according to his comrades) of being the first Ozark to receive a Purple Heart. Next day Pfc Clayton Richards, ASN 35545063, was killed in action, the first Ozark to die fighting for his country and ideals. Both of these men where members of Co I, 405th Infantry, which was then engaged near the small village of Waurichen.

Jim Hansen, 405-F

That night we moved up and relieved the infantry of the 2nd Armored division. Again my emotions ran amok. The 2nd and 3rd platoons went into prepared foxholes while the 1st platoon was to dig support foxholes in the rear. At this time, Lt. Rabinowitz was the 1st Platoon leader. He told Sgt. Matusiefsky to have his foxhole dug, while he reported to the CO. Sgt. Tom told him to dig his own damn foxhole, as we were in combat. This sorta started his long decline down the ladder of command success for Sgt. Tom.

Greenberg 405-F

Thursday, October 28.

When morning came I was able to see what was what. I had just finished spending my first night in the lines and had jumped for my rifle at every sound I heard. Grenades were always handy for instant use. I could see the pillbox behind me and was told it was to be the C.P. for our platoon. Three machine gun positions had been set up near us, taken from the 4th platoon. We did not set foot outside the foxhole during the day and just peeked out most of the time. In front we could see nothing and put more of our head up. Suddenly we heard something coming and ducked. It was German mortar shells coming in and some of them exploded near the pillbox. We kept our head down for awhile. An F.O. was put in the observation post of the pillbox. We ate "K" rations and used the wax boxes for urinating, etc. We were to do this many times before the war was over. Slept a little during the day. Went on guard during the night.

Greenberg 405-F
Friday, October 29.

About 5 A.M. -- food and water would be brought out to our holes. During the night in order to keep warm and being bored we improved our holes. Still it was funny compared to the super foxholes I would dig in the future. This hole was 5 feet deep, and 3 feet by 2 feet in width. We had learned this in basic but we learned they were no good in which to stay a few days. During the day we started crawling from one hole to another as we were lonely. We found that no one shot at us and we could see nothing so we started walking around with no one shooting at us. However when we heard a mortar shell coming in or going out we would dive for the hole. It took awhile for us to determine which were our shells going out and which were coming in. It would get dark about 5 P.M. when we started guard and did not get light till 7 A.M. We did not stand guard during the day but the long hours were killing us.

Greenberg 405-F
Saturday, October 30.

Something had to be done about these long hours with no sleep in the day and it was done. During the night two squads stood guard and one slept in the pillbox. In the daytime this squad would stand guard while one squad would go to the pillbox to rest and the other squad went back to Freylenberg for a good meal and a chance to wash up. This was rotated each day for a different squad. During the night a Yank tank hit a mine near us and started to burn and the shells inside started exploding. It burned all night. The crew was unharmed but the tank was rendered useless.

Greenberg 405-F
Sunday, October 31.

This morning was a bright day and wasn't raining for a change. The artillery liason planes were flying overhead when suddenly one dived for the ground followed by a German plane. Ack-ack came up and hit Jerry who went into flames and crashed. The liason plane was safe. At night we could hear fleets of Allied planes flying for hours over us on their way to Germany. Sometimes we could see bomb bursts on Cologne - 30 miles away. Once we saw a bomber burst into flames at night and crash. During the day P-47's and Mustangs flew around looking for Jerry in the air and on land.

Jim Hansen, 405-F

I don't recall all the events right after we were committed but we wound up in a small town surrounded by beet fields and cabbages. We ran patrols thru these fields day and night to try and intercept any German patrols that might have slipped thru our lines. One particular night we were between the beet fields when I stumbled upon my first dead German. I fell over his feet. I could see something glowing in the dark, on the ground. It was his teeth. Naturally I was nosey and, went to investigate. Upon closer investigation I discovered it was a man's mouth wide open and it was his teeth I had seen glowing in the moonlight. Then I discovered the rest of him. Due to the poor condition of the beet fields, I ran in place at least 10 minutes before getting away. When I finally got a grip on myself, I evacuated the area in a hurry. This was one of my worst moments so far in the early days of the war.

Greenberg, 405-F

Monday, November 1.

When our squad went to Freylenberg it was really a holiday. We were tired of "C" and "K" rations and a hot meal was worth the while. We left for Freylenberg before daylight and did not go back till dark as sometimes we were shelled. The town was small and there wasn't a building intact. The CO. kitchen, supply room, etc. were in basements. We ran around to the different houses picking up souvenirs and jars of preserved fruits in the basement. Naturally we always had our rifle, belt and gas mask even though there were no Germans in the town. We were always sorry to leave the ruins of Freylenburg.

Greenberg 405-F

Wednesday, November 10.

We moved up to Breyan Woods. This was a sector where there had been some fighting going on of late. We were relieving "E" Co. which had a few casualties. "E" Co. had smartened up and had built 2 man foxholes that we moved into. These holes that we were to always use in the future were about 5 feet deep, 8 feet long and 3-1/2 feet wide. A couple of doors are put over the hole and dirt on top. A narrow opening is left to stand guard. The doors and dirt was for protection against "time fire" and the weather. The hole was long enough to lie down on and two men allowed one to sleep while the other stood guard. Ammunition, grenades and rifle were on ledges near the opening ready for immediate use.

General Eisenhower visited the 102nd Division CP when it was located in the Hohenbusch Forest. Here he waves goodbye as he is accompanied to his jeep by General Keating. 10 November 1944.

Greenberg 405-F
Thursday, November 11

Up here things were indeed hotter. The weapons platoon with its mortars were just behind us and the German artillery was always trying to get them and we naturally kept low in our holes. Our platoon was in reserve up here and we were a little behind the 1st and 3rd platoons. We were already catching on to the "tricks of the trade". We were learning better ways to eat, sleep, rest and stand guard. We were seeing things that were hardening us for the future. Here and there were some bodies of German or American soldiers that have been dead for some time. A short distance from us was the body of a Jerry that had been run over by a tank - not a pleasant sight.

Greenberg 405-F
Saturday, November 13.

We had a little excitement early this morning. At 1 A.M. I was awakened by shooting. Hill was on guard at the time. It seemed two Germans had come in to surrender and had somehow passed thru the 1st and 3rd platoon lines. They came up to us yelling surrender. Molieu became excited and pumped a tracer between the legs of one of them who turned and ran the other remaining. The one running ran the length of the holes being shot at but not being hit. Lind however threw a grenade that brought him down. He was dead when they examined him. The other prisoner was brought to the rear for questioning. This incident caused us to be a little more alert for the rest of the night. It seems the longer the man stands guard the less alert he is. A man in combat a year is more careless on guard than one who has seen two months of combat.

At this point, November 13, 1944, Digger was reassigned from being an infantryman to a cook. The photographs of Digger's time in Germany and France are all from after this date. Presumably, there was little opportunity to take pictures while in an infantry unit on the front lines. Also, during this time Digger met Edwin Harwell, and based upon the photos sent home he and Harwell became close friends.

Digger and Harwell

"Harwell and Karnes by a waterfall- remember the song" (Digger)

Greenberg 405-F
Sunday, November 14.

Was lucky enough to win a pass. As we looked back at it, it was more a laugh than a pass as we were gone from dawn to darkness. It consisted of leaving about 5A.M. and walking back three miles where trucks picked up the four men from each CO. We arrived in time for a hot breakfast, the first we had eaten in a long time. We naturally always carried our rifle, belt and gas mask no matter where we went. At this rest center in Pallenberg we were able to wash and clean up and also get fresh clothing. We were able to write letters here and get some books to read and take back with us. We saw a movie in the afternoon and although it broke down a dozen times or more it was entertaining. After supper we took trucks back and walked the three miles to our holes and arrived just in time to stand our turn at guard.

Greenberg 405-F
Monday, November 15.

Came back to find a few things had occurred in my absence. Hill had been transferred to the 4th platoon and since I was on pass our hole had been unoccupied. In our absence a shell had landed right on the roof of it and that was that. I buddied up with Galloway and Brophy. Even though we did not have direct rifle fire occasionally at night stray bullets would come singing their merry way. Its not a pleasant sound to hear a bullet zing past although when you hear that sound you know that the bullet has missed you. It was one of these stray bullets that scratched Tideback just above the eye. It was a slight scratch and he didn't require any treatment but it was close. Some of the men seemed to be getting sick and about 4 or 5 were back in the hospital.

Greenberg 405-F
Saturday, November 20.

We left in a drizzling rain for Geilenkirken. We walked along the railroad most of the way as it led right into the city. A section of the Zigfried Line was built along the tracks. On one side of the tracks were lines of "dragon's teeth" that were tank obstacles. On the other side were some high cliffs that had pillboxes tucked in deep. As we were walking along the Engineers started blowing the pillboxes and bits of concrete and rocks started to fall among us. We dove into the ditches along the road and cursed the Engineers for about five minutes. We walked into Geilenkirken with rifles ready for action as snipers were still reported around. We selected a house and spent the night there.

"Now that ya mention it, it does sound like the patter of rain on a tin roof."

120. Willie and Joe cartoon from Stars and Stripes Newspaper (SSN)

The Ozark Division received orders for its first offensive mission on November 16. The objective was to seize the high ground near Prummern and Bauchem and the attack was planned as a two-day operation. During this period, the 102nd captured the towns of Immendorf, Apweiler, and Gereonsweiller. The battle for Immendorf occurred between 16-23 November and as an indication of the fierce fighting, nineteen soldiers from the 102nd Division earned the Silver Star Medal.

102nd thru Germany: WWII History 102nd Infantry Division

By 20 November Apweiler and Gereonsweiler had been seized by the 406th Infantry after 2d Armored Division's heavy slugging in the beet and grain fields around Immendorf. Colonel Hurless had expected to meet resistance in this area, but his doughboys were hardly prepared for the furious curtain of fire-which greeted them from pillboxes, machine guns, tanks and German 88's. Snipers lurked in every cellar, atop church steeples and on roofs. Bitter house-to-house fighting raged for hours. Topflight Panzer Grenadier and SS troops taking full advantage of community diggings, demolished buildings, anything that offered shelter, gave ground foot by foot.

However, the battle that was the cornerstone of this offensive was for the town of Beeck. Beeck was a strategic location in that the rapid advances of the 84th Division had left their flanks exposed. It was therefore necessary to seize the town of Beeck to eliminate this threat.

The 405th Regiment was assigned to capture the town. The 1st and 3rd Battalions were ordered to bypass Beeck to the east and seize the high ground to the north. The 2nd Battalion, including Company F, was to attack the town frontally. The Division narrative describes the battle in rather dry military prose, which refers to neutralizing heavy frontal machine gun fire, battling enemy Panzer tanks, and repulsing German counter attacks at great cost. Division narratives are written by staff officers secured far from the fighting. The battle for Beeck is better described by those infantry soldiers who fought in the cold, muddy beet fields, than by historians digesting the numbers after the fact.

Greenberg 405-F
Monday, November 22.

Early in the morning we awoke, ate a K ration and were given a couple bandoliers of ammo and a couple grenades. We were told our objective was to take Beeck -- a reg't objective. Co. F was to be in Battalion reserve. 1st Battalion on left, 3rd on right. It was raining as usual when we left Prummein. We walked up the road and then left it and were in wide-open country. We were deployed in formation -- spread out as much as possible. We could see tanks out in front blasting away. We kept on walking in rain and finally we were in enemy artillery range. Lindsey was hit by shrapnel in the face and had most of his teeth knocked out. Bleeding as he was, he walked around shaking our hands before going back to the rear for help. We jumped into foxholes as the tanks had been stopped.

The tanks were having a rough time and a few had been knocked out - we could see the British tank crews running back to safety. We kept moving up without tanks and passed a knocked out Jerry tank with burnt bodies in and around the tank. Heard E and G companies were having a rough time because of many pillboxes. We were committed and went around on the right flank. It was getting dark and 1st and 3rd platoons moved ahead -- suffered casualties and dug in for night - we did same. Am at no time giving Co. casualties, just platoon. Hoover was hit in leg. Still raining. Machine guns kept chattering all night and raining all night. While on guard in dark I saw a tank coming straight for the hole Coudra and I were in. I went out of hole and yelled for it to turn as I noticed it was a British tank -- It did. K rations were brought up at 4 A.M. -- after a sleepless night. It was still raining. Incident in afternoon. A few prisoners were captured and were walking back -- one wounded and complained he couldn't walk further. Parise went to look at him and a grenade fell off from his belt. The Jerry reached for it - Treifer, Clements and I shot him before he could pull pin.

Greenberg 405-F
Tuesday, November 23.

At 10 A.M. the 1st and 3rd platoon moved up and we did the same to take over their holes. Coudira, I and Molina moved up first. I saw bullets knocking up dirt at my feet and advised Coudira to hurry. I heard a yell behind me -- Molina had been killed instantly by a bullet thru his heart by sniper. Sniper kept shooting at us but we could not locate him. It was pouring rain. Our Thanksgiving dinner consisted of K ration. Told we would charge when tanks came up to support us. We put up smoke screen and Jerrys knew something was going to happen so he threw everything he had at us. Hell itself couldn't have been any worse. Our rifles were in sad shape -- so were we. Because of mud not one rifle in squad would fire. Tanks never showed up so we did not advance. Wrong order was given to 1st and 3rd plt. who advanced and had large casualties and had to retreat. We retreated also back to our holes of the morning -- still being shot at by sniper we couldn't locate. All afternoon we had heard the yells of a boy wounded about 100 yards in front of us. It was impossible to get to him. It was still raining. Stivali was hit coming back but it was only a scratch and he was OK. Ate K rations in holes and wondered what was going to happen now. Heard the C.O. was hit -- not bad. When it became dark we built new foxholes as the old ones were knee deep in water and mud. Thought we would get a bit of rest but didn't. The wounded had to be found and carried in. Carrying a wounded man is the hardest thing to do even for four men -- it wears you out in a few minutes and we weren't in tiptop shape in first place. A few fellows actually cried they were so -- tired. When we were finished with this and the hole we stood guard. It was still raining. It was this kind of living, especially standing in foxholes filled with water that gave some of us some new trouble. This trouble was trench foot. The first feeling of it is the feet getting cold and numb. A number of men were lucky to get it and go back to the hospital for a couple of months. Most of us thought we had it but our feet were just numb from the cold and if we did have it, it was just a slight case. Each of us three months later could pinch a toe and not have any feeling noticed.

Greenberg 405-F

Wednesday, November 24.

What was left of the Co. was relieved at 4 A.M. and we started back to Prummen. We were cold, tired, and hungry and it was raining and it was rough going in the mud and tank tracks. We passed stalled British tanks -- that is why they never came up to attack - the mud stopped them -- we also passed dead bodies. When we arrived we were given a slab of turkey and bread and a glass of rum. 50 of us slept in one cellar as shells were coming into the town. Our platoon had been lucky in casualties. The 1st and 3rd had suffered 12 dead and about 40 wounded. Lt. Huff had a tree fall on his back. E Co. had 56 men left and G Co. was no better off. Both Co.'s had most of their officers either killed or wounded. We went to sleep, cramped as we were and dead tired. The 3rd. plt. medic had been badly hit.

Thanksgiving Dinner
Two Ozark infantrymen, Pfc William G. Curtis from San Diego, California, and Pfc Donald R. Stratton from Colville, Washington, enjoy a hasty meal in the battered window of a shell-torn house far, far from home. 23 November 1944, Waurichen, Germany.

Jim Hansen, 405-F

Our next objective was Beeck. F. Co. was to make a frontal attack. G. Co. was on the right and a British unit was on the left. As we came out of a small valley we were about 300 yards from a little town. Then all hell broke loose and we dove into fox holes the

Germans had dug. We couldn't go forward a foot -- the fire was that intense. I raised my head a little for a look see -- and the Germans fired an 88 at me and the tank behind me. The shell passed directly over my head and the muzzle blast was so severe it tore my helmet off my head and deposited it beside my fox hole. I was in fairy land, for a few minutes. As Lt. Greene and Sgt. Tom were both gone, the Capt. again put me in charge of the platoon. I called the platoon leaders back for a short meeting. I crawled about 50 yards before I was below the crest of a small hill.

After the meeting we had to get back to our platoon and get ready for a move out about 5 PM. As I reached the crest of the hill I rested for a minute before I made a dash for my foxhole. I took off as fast as I could. Almost immediately I was aware of a terrific explosion and I just sort a faded away.

I had been hit in the head. The force of the bullet and the steel helmet, being ripped from my head put me to sleep for a while. When I came too, every few seconds I would feel something tugging at the back of my pack on my back. I became aware of the crack of a bullet every time I felt the tugging. Actually, it was the bullets going thru my mess kit in my pack. As I raised my head to look around I saw faces I recognized. They were watching me and they were smiling. My men thought I had bought it and that I was dead. I told them to open fire and I would make a run for my fox hole. This they did, and I made the hole. I was bleeding, but it was nice to be in a hole now. There was a small haystack directly to our front. A few tracer bullets finally set it afire. A sniper jumped out of the haystack, and both platoons opened fire on that SOB.

It was time to attack again. It was almost dark now. Again the German resistance was terrific. The Germans were not ready to move out of Beeck. The British tanks had moved up to our rear and were firing their 75's and heavy machine guns at the town. They had not pulled far enough up the hill and were firing thru our troops and hitting our own men. I jumped up on a tank and yelled for them to cease fire -- as they were killing Americans. I was as mad as a hornet. I told the tank commanders, "If that's the best you can do, get the hell out of here." And so, they did.

Jim Hanson's experience with the sniper bullet going through his helmet is also related by Dick Skene.

Dick Skene, 405-F

Here we were again to move in and take over for the 84th Division defensive positions, with the idea of possibly conducting a frontal assault on the small town of Beeck itself later on. We hiked what seemed like miles across mud, through beet fields. The going was pretty tough. I recall coming up on a small hillside, after we had been intermittently shelled by mortar fire and seeing Capt. Peterson there, looking over the front lines with some of the members of his staff. Also, once we had passed beyond Capt. Peterson and his people, we suddenly came under fire from a sniper. We raced forward to occupy the foxholes that were laying just ahead of us, and in the process, John Stivali, who was close to me, was hit in the wrist with a bullet. Three of us ended up in one foxhole, that was Bill Veet, John Stivali, and myself, and Bill set about using his first aide packet to wrap up John's wrist. The sniper who had been shooting at us had been shooting some tracer shots and we had an idea, approximately, where he was. It also turned out he had shot and killed another of our group, Molina. But we did not find out about this until later. The three of us in the foxhole, after getting John's wrist bandaged up stayed low, kept our noses in the mud, stayed out of the line of fire from the sniper. About this time, Jim Hanson came up to our hole and was standing right beside the foxhole before any of us realized it. As I turned and saw him, and started to yell for him to get down, one of the sniper's bullets, a tracer, passed thru the raincoat that was on the small pack that was on his back. Jim dropped to his knees and about the time he dropped to his knees, another bullet came across and hit him in the helmet. He dropped down -- he'd been hit. But the bullet apparently had entered the helmet, pretty well torn up the inside of the helmet liner, the top part, and gone out without seriously wounding Jim Hanson. That was about as close a call as anyone could hope to survive. I don't think we would get much disagreement if we said that Beeck was bad news to the 405th Infantry Regiment.

During the next operation by the Ozark Division, they spearheaded the drive to the Roer River in the Linnich area. The attack began for the 405th on the night of 26 - 27 November. The German line of battle included the 10th SS Panzer Division plus attached units. The following paragraph describing the 2nd Battalion and F Company attack on Linnich was marked in Digger's copy of the Division history. As this is the only passage highlighted in the book, I can only assume this particular action held some significance for Digger.

The low ridge afforded some protection from emplacements to the east and northeast down the long slope toward Linnich and it was not until the battalion crossed this rise and was on the way to the objective that the enemy opened fire. Further progress resolved into a process of slowly creeping from anthill to anthill at the rate of 150 yards in two hours. Fire gradually increased so that further movement over the naked terrain was impossible. It wasn't until December 2nd that the battle for Linnich was finally over.

Greenberg 405-F
Tuesday, November 30.

We were told we would leave the trench and walk for a mile and then attack. We started leaving about 6:30 A.M. and just before our platoon and the M.G. section Germans started firing at us. It seems a platoon of Germans infiltrated during the night, and they were in GERCEVICH the brush. A machine gunner was killed getting out. We left the trench firing at the Germans as a Co. of tanks came up to rescue us. They went right thru us to where the Germans were and cut them to ribbons. Our platoon had two casualties -- Wright -- hit in arm and Patrick in leg. Parada and Taverez became sick and went to hospital. We went over to our place of attack, rested half an hour and then attacked some German pillboxes. We couldn't get them and suffered casualties. 1st platoon suffered most casualties again -- 3 killed and 10 wounded. We were lucky - only one casualty - Blyskeel hit in arm by shrapnel. We dug in.

German propaganda messages loaded into artillery shells and fired into Roerdorf were addressed to the "Boys of the 102d" and "To the poor Devils of the 102d". The Ozarks' only gripe concerned the fact that there never were enough leaflets to go around. As souvenirs, demand far exceeded supply.

The following excerpt from Gene Greenberg's diary is perhaps the most intense of this entire narrative. But by late November, the men of the 405th were battled hardened veterans, and consequently, the description of this incident is rather mundane.

Greenberg 405-F
Saturday, November 27.

The previous morning, I had myself in a near tragedy. It was about 7 in the morning and Munger and Clements had just relieved me. I was wrapped on my ledge fast asleep. Since it was just about daylight they decided to go back for some coffee in the pillbox where the C.P. was. At that time 5 Germans jumped into the shallow part of the trench and started moving down the trench. They threw a grenade and it landed on a ledge of the trench just above me and exploded. This woke me up and the first thing I heard was someone talking in German. I couldn't move or see anything as I had wrapped myself tightly in blankets. I felt someone brush against me -- it was the Jerry who had slipped. He started firing his sub -- machine gun right over my head as he was standing only a few feet away from me. The Jerry was probably just as scared as me and probably thought I was a blanket roll. The other fellows were awake by this time and making it hot for Jerry who decided to run for it. However one was killed. I was OK but scared beyond words. All the other fellows thought I was dead because they told me Jerry was standing just where I lay. Later in the day a 2-1/2 inch piece of shrapnel bounced off my leg and didn't even scratch me.

Dick Skene, 405-F

Another incident that comes to mind is moving into another one of the defensive trenches to relieve someone else. The people we relieved advised us that at the other end of the trench was a cement bunker or pillbox, still occupied by the Germans. We only occupied the portion of the trench that really led up to the German positions. We had moved into this position during the daytime and had a chance to look around a little bit. We could see the German pillbox, but we saw no signs of activity. The area was generally inactive, and reasonably quiet. I do recall that Col. Bishoft, commanding officer of the 3rd battalion, came up to check things out in our positions up there. We kind of leisurely settled into this new position, enlarged a foxhole leading off the trench, so we could lie down when it came time to take a little snooze. Some of us took off our gear, which included my canteen, and laid it up on the side of the trench. We posted guards and took the usual turns at night. Come the early dawn, all hell broke loose. A German patrol, apparently thinking the Americans had pulled out, had come on down the trench line, ostensibly from the pillbox that they still held, and got in amongst the troops in the trench. I heard that one of the German soldiers actually fell over Greenburg, who was a member of the 2nd platoon. Everybody was scrambling for weapons, and pretty soon everybody was shooting. Capt. Weygan showed up near our foxhole, hollering and yelling and shooting along with the rest of us. I don't even know how many people were wounded on our side or the Germans in that little encounter. I think it was pretty much a standoff, and in the surprise and confusion of the whole episode, there was probably very few people injured. I do recall, after the mess was over with and we halfway settled down, reaching up to get my gear that had been put on the side of the trench, which included my canteen. The canteen wasn't much good anymore, it was full of holes.

87b. Destruction to a German City (VR)

1st platoon 405th (Digger)

2nd Platoon 405th (Digger)

3rd Platoon 405th (Digger)

4th platoon 405th (Digger)

After the capture of Linnich, the soldiers of the 102nd often wondered why the 9th Army didn't just keep going and capture the high ground across the Roer River. Instead, the American troops moved up to the west bank of the Roer River and occupied defensive positions, while the Germans strengthened their defenses on the far side of the river. The 102nd, like the other Divisions on the front during this period, was at the far end of a very tenuous supply line. There were shortages of ammunition, including grenades, and equipment. Overshoes and shoepacs also needed to be procured for the upcoming offensive. In short, without additional supplies of food, ammunition, and equipment, the offensive effort required to breech the Roer River on a broad front simply was not feasible.

The Division history notes: "On December 16, 1944, German General Von Runstead attacked without warning in the Malmedy-Bastone sector some fifty miles south of the positions held by the 102nd Division." The Battle of the Bulge had begun. "The Ninth Army abandoned all plans for an early crossing of the Roer River and began shifting troops to the First Army area in an effort to bolster their defense. The changes directly and quickly affected the Ozark Division, when on December 20, the 84th Infantry Division was withdrawn from its position on the 102nd Division left flank." Consequently, the Ozarks now defended an area previously occupied by two divisions.

(Digger)

Jim Hansen, 405-F

The Battle of the Bulge cranked up. Whole divisions were pulled out of the lines and shipped to the rear to get in front of the Germans. Great gaps existed all along our front. We settled into a defensive mode. We began the job of making fox holes livable. Empty artillery shell cases were driven down in the ground at an angle to support a solid roof. The fox holes were dug so both men could lie down and sleep. Little pot bellied stoves were located and installed with complete chimneys. Coal was plentiful and hauled to each hole at night. It was really quite warm when the opening was closed. Guard rosters were made up so a minimum of men were needed to do guard duty. The BAR's were in each fox hole. Barbed wire was placed about in front of our positions. The BAR's were fired quite often to keep them from freezing and to discourage any Germans from sneaking in. Everyone said that the first platoon was trigger happy but no patrols got in on us. We got a new Capt. as an observer at this time. He had been relieved from his company and sent back for a retread job. He came to my CP one morning which was in the basement of a wrecked house. He was all excited and wanted to know if I knew that smoke was coming out of every fox hole in the 1st platoon? I said, "Yes Sir., and from the 2nd, 3rd, 4th and all the weapons platoon positions as well." He said, "Don't you know that you are giving away their locations to the enemy?" I said, "Capt., the Germans know where we are and we know where they are. We don't bother them and they don't bother us."

When the Battle of the Bulge was turning in our favor, we began cleaning out the last pockets of resistance on the west bank of the river. We captured most of a Bn. of Germans and finally got the Bn. Commander, too. His job was to keep us busy so we couldn't go help the men fighting the Bulge. SS troops were assigned to his unit to see that his orders were carried out and also to see that none of the men crossed over to our side. This didn't help any as we captured the SS men too.

Greenberg 405-F

Saturday, December 25, 1944

We had spent Xmas Eve on guard but we had a little party when we came into the pillbox after being relieved. The Lt. had opened two bottles of whiskey that was part of his liquor ration and we all had a slug. During Xmas Day we received quite an artillery barrage but most of them were duds and were filled with propaganda leaflets. Our kitchen was in Pollck and by squads we went back there to eat our turkey Xmas dinner. This meal was different from most meals in that we ate till we were ready to bust and then we were given turkey and bread to take back to the pillboxes so that we could eat later if we wished. Later in the day we saw an American artillery cub shot down by a Jerry fighter plane.

Greenberg 405-F
Sunday, December 26.

At this time the Germans were pushing ahead in the Bulge and the whole 9th Army except the 102nd and 29th div. and some tank destroyer units were sent down to protect our southern flank. Naturally when there are only two divisions left to take care of the whole 9th army sector we were spread quite thin. During the day there was a great deal of activity. We kept digging line after line of foxholes. The engineers kept putting up barbed wire and mine fields in front of these holes. The heavy weapons and the anti-tank guns dug positions too. When we finished our line of defense, we would move back a short distance and dig another line of fortifications. If the Germans chose to attack they would not find us too strong. At night the tank destroyers would roll up and down the roads at night just to give the Germans the impression that we had a great deal of armor and that we were getting prepared for an offensive. What we didn't know at the time was that the Germans has sent all their available reserves down to the Bulge and that they were doing the same as us -- digging fortifications in view of a possible attack by us.

Greenberg 405-F
Wednesday, December 29.

This morning some of us decided to view the battlefield at Beeck where our reg't had been cut to pieces and where we had sustained extremely heavy casualties. It made us feel funny to see equipment bearing the names of fellows who had been killed or wounded. We also had an opportunity to stand in the German's position and see how we must have looked when attacking and we came to the conclusion that we were pretty lucky to be alive. When we came back we were told another patrol was to go out on "recon". All those who hadn't gone the previous evening drew straws. Again I wasn't picked. We were all extremely happy when they returned safe in the morning.

Greenberg 405-F
Monday, January 4.

The whole company was going back to Holland to take a shower. This was quite a job. First we would be given some clean clothing and a towel which we wouldn't put on till we returned from the shower. Then when ready to go we would assemble outside with rifle, belt and toilet articles. We would then start walking about three miles back to where we got the trucks. The trucks couldn't advance any nearer as they were afraid to attract artillery. It was pretty cold and when we finally arrived at the coal mine in Holland we were frozen. We had a hot shower, shaved and then went back to Prummein in the same manner that we left.

Col. Biddle, Lt. Col. Woodruff, Major Winters, Capt. Ledgerwood, Capt. Peterson, Capt. Everson, Lt. Weigand (Digger)

On January 26, the Ozark Division initiated an attack against one of the most highly organized defensive sectors of the famous West Wall. This area contained a very high concentration of closely integrated and mutually supporting concrete pillboxes. These defenses were an average of one mile in depth and contained at least eighty major pillboxes. The Division history states,

"Appreciating the futility of frontally attacking the nest of concrete and steel pillboxes, sited in depth in three general lines and all mutually supporting by fire, the Division scheme of maneuver was to envelop them from the flanks and rear." The Division engineers began converting thousands of pounds of TNT into satchel charges for use in destroying the enemy emplacements.

The attack commenced on January 26th with the 407th Regiment attacking the town of Brachelen. The 405th was to advance on the Division's left flank at H plus 60, or 60 minutes after the 407th began its attack. Expecting heavy casualties, the Ozarks advanced into what had been enemy territory and found it all but abandoned. Thus, the last German defenses west of the Roer River fell with a whimper rather than a bang.

The 405th was given a two-day pass back across the border in Holland. The showers, movies and relaxation were much appreciated, but Gene Greenberg's comment on the great number of supplies stockpiled for the Roer River crossing left little doubt the war was far from over.

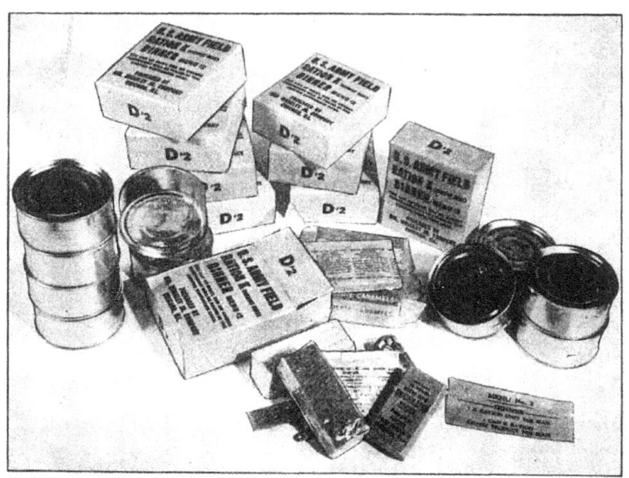

Field Ration 10 in 1

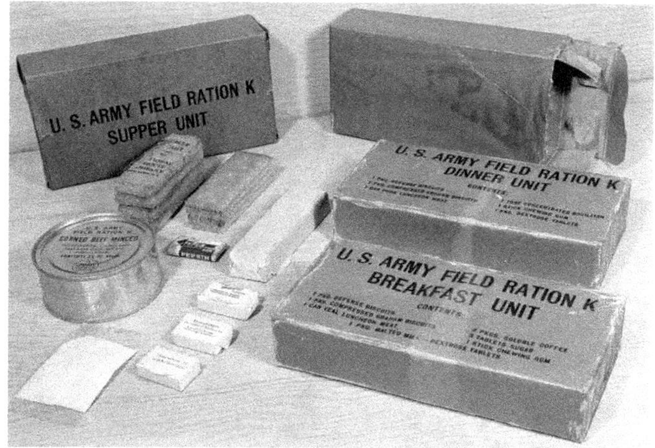

K Ration

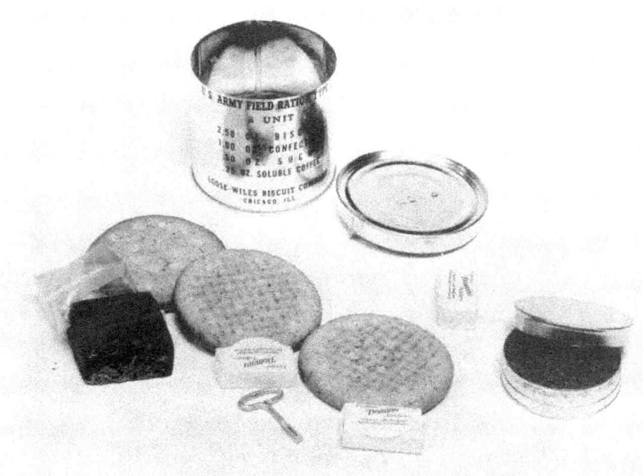

1941 C Ration

The military must have produced an amazing number of C Rations because I was issued Cs manufactured in 1944, when I joined the Air Force in 1975. We ate these until MREs were introduced in the early 1980s.

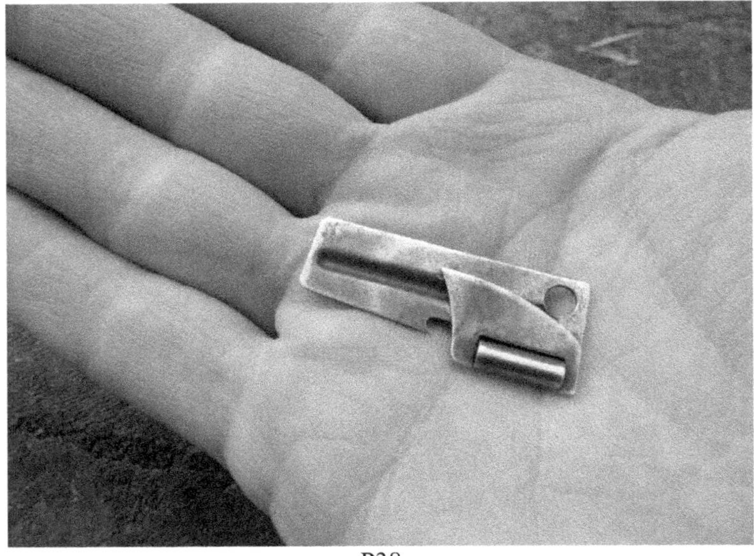

P38
You would go hungry without one of these P38 can openers. Generations of US military personnel had one of these hanging on their dog tags.

Greenberg 405-F
Saturday, January 30.

We were having a pretty good time here just resting and eating. A large number of packages plus mail arrived so we were far from unhappy. We wrote letters in the day room and listened to the radio. The food wasn't too good, but we weren't complaining. We took a shower about twice a day just because we felt so good. Besides, we had noticed on the way here, and I had noticed on my pass to Herleen that for miles the sides of the roads were lined with every kind of ammunition available plus great quantities of food. We weren't too sure when we would get our next shower.

Greenberg 405-F
Tuesday, February 2.

Today we were told why we were brought back for a rest -- and we learned it was not going to be a very good rest. The 102nd div. had been chosen to lead the 9th Army across the Roer River and our reg't had been chosen to lead the division. Each platoon was brought down to regimental HQ where there was a sand table showing just where the Co. was going to cross, what grounds and towns it was to take. We were shown where minefields were supposed to be. We were shown aerial photographs of the terrain and we were assured that it wasn't going to be an easy job.

Greenberg 405-F
Thursday, February 4.

We were told that tomorrow we would go back to Holland and practice on a small river how to cross in assault boats. We spent the rest of the morning listening to lectures and further information regarding arial photographs that had been taken recently of the Roer River. It's surprising how much one can actually see in these photographs. One thing was conspicuously absent - pillboxes. When we had reached the Roer River we had broken thru the Zigfried line in its entirety. On the other side of the Roer was the Cologne plain to the Rhine. We were issued life preservers.

Greenberg 405-F
Saturday, February 6.

We learned the plan of attack for the crossing of the Roer. The 405th and the 407th were to attack and 405th reg't, the 1st battalion, would cross first, we of the 2nd battalion would follow and then the 3rd battalion. The 1st battalion would cross first, gain some high ground and we would go thru them capturing the town of Tetz. In the second battalion the order of crossing would be "E", "F", "G", and "H". "F" co. was to keep contact with the 29th div. and flank Tetz while "E" entered the town. We could expect no armor for two days to support us and were to go as far forward as possible

Greenberg 405-F
Sunday, February 7.

The company received a number of replacements and our squad received three of them. Ybarra was a Mexican kid from Arizona who had been a cook until transferred to the Infantry. Nolan had been transferred from a clerk's job in division up to us. He was married and had two kids. Ravera came from the Lower East Side, had just arrived from the States. He was only 18 years old and a good-looking fellow. None of the three had seen combat. All three were to drown when attempting to cross the Roer River. We felt sorry for them when we received them in our squad cause they were stepping into the thick of it without any previous experience.

Greenberg 405-F
Monday, February 8.

It was during the night that we heard something flying with a loud noise outside. First we thought it was a Jerry plane but when looking outside we saw a fire in the sky that passed overhead with the speed of a plane. It had the most weird and powerful noise. We knew that it was a V-1 and as long as we heard the noise we were safe. We were to become used to this noise and during the day we could see the V-1's fly over in twos and threes in formation. We could see during the daytime that the V-1s looked like airplanes with short wings. We heard they usually dropped in Antwerp or London.

Greenberg 405-F
Thursday, February 11.

We were told the next morning that we had been alerted and that we might cross the Roer any evening. The "Stars and Stripes" quoted the Germans as saying they expected the attack just where we were, so we knew that we couldn't surprise them. During the day we had nothing to do, so we would steal the 10-in-1s off the armored cars in the vicinity and put the empty 10-in-1 box back. We could imagine the tankers and the armored outfit men cursing us when they looked for something to eat. We did this for three days and for three days we weren't hungry. Naturally this was plus our usual meals.

Planning continued for the Roer River crossing. The Ninth Army had been chosen to make the attack, and the 102nd Division was to be the lead element. The Ozark's plan for the crossing operation was to attack with two regimental combat teams abreast. The 405th would cross at Flossdorf and Rurdorf while the 407th crossed at Linnich. The attack was codenamed *Operation Grenade* and was scheduled to commence on February 10. However, on February 9, the Germans damaged the floodgates on the Roer River dams located in the highlands south of Duren.

An excerpt from The Office of Medical History document *From the Roer to the Elbe* describes the situation after the Roer River Dams are destroyed.

"The flood caused by the damaged dams resulted in the river rising an average of 5 feet and increasing in width, depending on the terrain, to between 400 and 1,200 yards. The river's velocity increased to an average speed of ten and a half feet per second--all of which made rafting operations virtually impossible. The resultant delay, while disappointing, allowed the army staff to refine their plans and to increase their stockpiles of supplies and ammunition."

It would take approximately two weeks for the river to reach something approaching the natural stream flow at that season. D-Day for Operation Grenade was therefore moved to February 20.

Greenberg 405-F
Saturday, February 13.

We were given some news that made us happy. The Germans had blown up the dams above the Roer River and now this stream was a raging torrent impossible to cross. We were to return to Baisweiler that night. We knew that we would have to cross the river at a later date but we felt that there was a chance that orders might be changed and we would not have to cross the river. We were in good spirits while packing our belongings. However our high spirits were slightly dampened on the return trip to Baisweiler because all our feet were killing us due to the new overshoes we had been given.

Greenberg 405-F
Thursday, February 18.

We left in the morning to train again for river crossings. This time we were taken to the Maas River near Liege. This river is not small by any means - about 400 yards wide and there was a swift current. We had our packs on our back and life preservers around us. Our squad took off in the boat and by the time we crossed we had been pushed downstream about 300 yards and were quite tired. We pulled the boat upstream and crossed again. That was all we had to do for the day and it was quite enough. It was already starting to get dark when we boarded the trucks and we arrived back in Baisweiler about 9 P.M.

Greenberg 405-F
Monday, February 22.

Finally it had come. We were told that we were going to take off at 2 A.M the next morning and to get all our equipment ready. For the rest of the day fellows were cleaning rifles, writing letters, packing equipment or just laying around trying to sleep. The new fellows were nervous but I imagine the old fellows felt no better. I know I didn't. A big mail call helped build up our morale. We went to sleep at 6 P. M. because we would be getting up around midnight. We took turns staying awake so that we would not oversleep.

All battles are undoubtedly considered important by those who fight them, but the Roer River crossing was the 102nd Division's most notable engagement, and it was also one of the most important campaigns of the European theater in WWII. The following excerpt was written by journalist Howard K. Smith while he was a war correspondent attached to C Company of the 405th.

102nd thru Germany: WWII History 102nd Infantry Division

To these men must go the credit. Their story is well told by Howard K. Smith, CBS correspondent who lived with the men in those tense first hours of the great Allied offensive which marked the beginning of Germany's end. His diary records the great moments and the sacrifices of only a few individuals who were responsible for our victory. To record them all would fill volumes.

Howard K. Smith

0315 hours:

This is Roerdorf and I am in a deep strong cellar, thank God. I don't think I shall ever again witness a spectacle as terrifying as that I have just seen.

We marched over the silent road to a village called Welz, halfway to the river. When we were leaving the village, our barrage opened up at precisely 0245 hours. Almost instantly the navy blue sky turned into a dome of yellow fire as a thousand guns blasted forth. And they kept on firing, dotting the horizons behind and in front of us with momentary patches of red from the blasts of the guns and the hits of our shells. They thundered and roared over our heads like a hundred express trains. On that flat plain, walking erect, I felt naked, exposed, terrified. Once I think I almost broke. I wanted to dive for the ditch and stay in it until this was over. But I looked ahead and saw Pancho strutting on like a bantam rooster and I was ashamed of myself. This is what I mean by saying company and platoon leaders mold the shape of war. If Pancho had shown a sign of breaking, I'd have gone into the ditch to stay. And I think a lot of soldiers would have gone with me.

Jerry was apparently stunned by the sudden blast. He did not respond for a full quarter hour. Then he cut loose. Among other things, he lined our road with mortar bursts. Three times I had to dive for the ditch. Once I lost my helmet and spent a terrible minute groping in the mud for it.

We left the road and cut across the fields, a long twisting snake of moving men, all following Pancho. Then our long-range machine guns opened up from a thousand foxholes behind us, firing shoulder-level tracers, chains of bright purple lights, toward Jerry's lines on the river. We had to fall on our hands and knees and crawl to escape our own murderous fire.

At the road running parallel to the river, I shouted an inaudible "Good luck!" and ran down the road to the first house in Roerdorf. I was in the cellar in nothing flat. It turned out to be the headquarters of the combat engineers, who are out there in that inferno, trying to put up a pontoon bridge. Meanwhile the first wave of the infantry is crossing in boats -- in all of them except boat No. 13.

0400 hours:

Colonel Robert Anderson of Boise, Idaho, is the commander of the 327th Engineers, who are doing this job and whose headquarters this cellar is. Yesterday, when I interviewed him about his plans for the bridges, he was a picture of poise. Now he chain-smokes and drinks mug after mug of hot black coffee. He has a hard job -- probably the hardest job -- to do today. His men must put up the bridges to supply and reinforce the infantry. He must do it on sites zeroed in by German guns for months. The Army Manual says you cannot build a pontoon bridge in a river with a current of more than five miles an hour. The current at Roerdorf is more than six miles an hour.

The bridge in the vicinity of Roerdorf is not doing well to understate the situation. The engineers on the flaming riverbank are losing the boats, which are to be used as pontoons, and the boats are cruising off down the river. Some of the boats Anderson had loaned to the infantry to use as assault craft have been capsizing in the driving stream and floating off. There is now a shortage of boats for pontoons. Colonel Anderson has sent for more. Meanwhile crews are out farther down along the river, trying to salvage the runaway boats.

Anderson himself has just put on his helmet and gone down to the riverbank. His communications are shot to hell. Most of his wires have been cut by German artillery, which is plowing the riverbank and the village.

0430 hours:

I tried to write this in the medical aid station I just visited down the street. But the little house was overflowing with wounded, and I had to leave.

The floor of the main room was sticky with mixed blood and dust. Men with legs broken and purple were lying on stretchers. There were others with their sides gashed wide open. One man was torn up terribly everywhere. Were it not for the tension, I think I would be sick. Being scared, tired, and confused has some advantages, and this is one of them. Outside on the streets a deep black night is closing in. I ran from cover to cover until I reached the place where this is being written: the command post of 405th Regiment, in another cellar. This front-line village has certainly altered in appearance during the last hour. I noticed more and more great gaps where houses used to be. And I can hear others rumbling to rubble following blasts all over town. If the infantry doesn't soon push Jerry back to where his mortars can't reach this town, there will be nothing left above ground.

Here in the CP, I have run into a combat fatigue case. His name is not Walt, but that will serve. He was out on the riverbank repairing telephone lines when an 88 hit his buddy right in the back. Walt, a giant of a man, is now sitting on the floor here, crying like a baby. His jacket is splattered with blood and tiny bits of flesh. He is uncontrollable and should be evacuated from the zone of fire. The medics say, though, that there are other men who may die if they are not evacuated immediately, and Walt must wait. I tried to talk to him, but he didn't hear a word I said.

0600 hours:

I have spent an hour with the commander of the regiment, a gaunt white-haired colonel named Williams. His eyes are inflamed from lack of sleep. He planned the attack last night and is making it tonight. His hands tremble as he points to places on the map.

"It's the damned bridges," he explained. "We can't get one to stay in that current. It cuts them in half like a band saw. We've got a battalion of infantry on the other side, without supplies and not enough ammunition to last the day out."

There is one bridge up now, but it can't stand a load until an auxiliary cable is thrown across. The infantry are still crossing in what boats they can get. And they're still capsizing and finally reaching shore a mile down the river, wet, cold, uncertain of mines in that unreconnoitered area.

Colonel Williams had called for Alligators, to carry his men over faster, before the Germans could counterattack. Eight Gators were on the way. Not enough. But there were other crossing sites, and they, too, were clamoring for Gators.

There is no word from C Company and Pancho.

0800 hours:

This is an artillery observation post in Roerdorf, in the shattered attic of a three-story house. Though it is dawn, I can see nothing but the vague outlines of the high ground across the river, and flashes and tracer bullets. A rather thick ground haze covers the horizon.

Captain Jack Potts of Corsicana, Texas, the regiment's front-line artillery observer, asks me why the hell I stay out in this if I don't have to. Now that I think of it, it does seem rather silly. I am no hero and every minute of this has been torture to me. But also it's fascinating.

1000 hours:

The mortar shelling let up a little and I went down to the bridge site. It was not hard to find, for the zigzag road was marked by great patches of blood on the plowed earth, by smashed canteens, ripped jackets, splintered rifle butts, and general destruction. It has been an awful night out there.

But the bridge is up. The second cable is being fastened on the other side now. Troops are lining the streets in town, waiting to cross. Meanwhile, upstream, the Alligators are taking others over. We have lost two Alligators this morning.

1100 hours:

The worst has happened. When the bridge was almost complete, one of the Alligators upstream got out of hand in the current. It smashed the bridge and broke both cables.

That is not all. The liberated pontoon boats rushed downstream, where they collided with another pontoon bridge a mile away, and shattered that one as well. Colonel Anderson is in misery. My head aches and I am going to try to sleep in the engineers' cellar.

There is one heartening thing, though: For the first morning in weeks, the sky is cloudless. The air is roaring with fighter-bombers. We can see them peeling off into dives, see their guns flashing and hear their tattoo. They will help those weary battered infantrymen on the other side.

1300 hours:

Colonel Anderson has come in and is sitting on a blanket in this cellar room. He says German artillery ceased hitting the riverbank an hour ago. The bridge will be completed within a couple of hours. Work has already begun on another, heavier bridge. It will carry tanks and heavy guns to support the infantry.

1400 hours:

It's a warm, sunny, spring like day outside. I walked back down to the regimental CP without fear. Jerry's mortars have been pushed way back and can't reach us any more. His artillery can, but apparently the infantry on the other side are giving it enough to do over there.

Sic infit – and so it begins, for the men of the 405th. These are their tales of one of the most significant and deadly battles of WWII in Europe.

Greenberg 405-F

Tuesday, February 23.

We awoke at midnight, had a hot meal, put on our equipment, shook hands with one another, wishing luck, etc. and went outside awaiting orders to move. At 2 A.M. we started down the road with very little talking among the men. We walked about a mile before reaching Edern. It was a clear night without a moon and wasn't a bad night for a crossing. As we left Edern and approached Welz the artillery started. This was really something. It seemed as if every large gun in the American Army was firing. The 155s and the 105s were booming behind us. We had passed them and seen and heard the firing orders. In front of us 75s, tanks, antitank guns, all types of mortars, cannons, and machine guns were firing. The noise was terrific and we could see the explosions of phosphorous shells on the other side of the river and tracer bullets from machine guns flying in an arc toward the other side of the stream. In Welz we were given more bandoleers and grenades we were soon near Roerdorf. Tanks and bulldozers moved up on the roads. Just outside of Roerdorf we halted and heard the Engineers had tried putting up a footbridge but suffered too many casualties. There was some confusion as to what units were going first but that was straightened out and we moved thru the town to the river. We approached the river and were on a small hill overlooking it. A winding road for about 100 yards led down to the boats. We stopped on the top of this road when all hell broke loose. The Jerrys had the place zeroed in and big artillery shells started dropping around us. A big one fell about 50 yards in front of me and I could hear screaming and moaning of the wounded. Another fell much closer and it seemed everyone was hit. All around us medics, engineers, and infantrymen lay dead or wounded. Galloway was beside me when he was hit in the hip and the foot. I brought him back to the medics and returned. Lt. Fletcher had been hit in the head but not badly. Overman had been hit in the arm and was evacuated. A bulldozer was repairing the road and bodies were pushed aside by the dozer. There was still a great deal of wounded, bleeding, dead and confused men around. E Co. just in front of us had a whole platoon wiped out. Remember all the time it was dark. What was left of us moved down to the boats and our platoon was to cross in three boats. Our squad jumped in a boat when there were three engineers and took off. The current was swift, the engineers excited, too few people paddling and perhaps too many men in the boat, but we were out of control and the boat was being swept down the river without being able to do anything about it. The boat hit all kinds of objects and we approached a dam with a large hole in it -- out boat passed thru the dam and kept going. Suddenly the boat hit a submerged log and split the boat in two. We jumped out into the cold water. This was about 5 A.M. It was dark but my preserver helped little and I felt a branch in my hand and held on. I moved up on the branch till I came to a strong part and just held on exhausted. I was in water up to my neck and held on for dear life. I could hear other fellows calling for help and could see empty battered boats passing. Artillery shells were falling in the river and machine gun bullets passed overhead. I was forced to get under the water at times because of this. Everything seemed so unreal. I started taking off my equipment. My rifle and helmet was gone and I removed my overshoes, pack, belt, rations, ammo bag with grenades, 3 bandoleers, raincoat and kept the life preserver. My legs were numb and I worked myself up to where the water was up to my chest. As dawn came, I was conscious of someone else holding on the tree at the opposite end. I called out and found out it was Bilyk. I crawled up to where Bilyk was, as it was higher out of the water. Bilyk told me he was in the boat with the 3rd squad and their boat had turned over just like our boat did. It started to get light but there was a thick fog descending which prevented visibility for more than 20 ft. The fog aided us from enemy fire but prevented us from being rescued. We were freezing and as I looked at Bilyk I thought there were two of him he was shaking so. I brought out a small bottle of whiskey that my parents had sent in a package and which I and the squad had agreed to save till we crossed the river as we thought we would be cold. Well we hadn't crossed the river but we were cold, so we finished it. Bilyk had thought I had gone nuts when I told him I had whiskey. We finished it we kept holding on and freezing. There was no more firing so we figured our boys had pushed on - we hoped. It would be bad for us if the Germans were still on the other side of the river when the fog lifted. After 3-1/2 hours we heard someone talking on our side of the river. We both called and the voice answered saying he was going for help. The fog was too thick to see him. After 20 minutes a boat suddenly appeared out of the mist -- no one in it, but a rope was attached to it. Our rescuers were trying to get the boat to us and then tow us in -- the current was too rapid for them to paddle out. After one half hour trying we were finally rescued. We were taken to a First Aid station where we were warmed by a fire and given dry clothing.

We ate a K ration and after being out of the river five hours we were on our way back to rejoin our co. We walked down the same winding road where the shells had first dropped and in the light of day could see what had happened. The road was literally red and equipment was scattered all about. A footbridge had been erected and a pontoon bridge was being built. American wounded were being carried back by Jerry prisoners and Yank dead lined the road - some not in one piece. On all sides of the road were mine fields. When I reached the Co. I found that Tetz, our first objective, had been taken. I also learned the casualties - from my boat only I and Brophy, who had drifted to safety were safe. Taverez, Ybarra, Burke, Nolan, Ravera, White, Coudia and two engineers were missing in action. Later after the war was over we learned that Burke and White had been taken prisoner. In Bilyk's boat Tom White, Veit, Stivali, Wingate, Sloan, and Dryer were missing. Weit also turned up as a prisoner of war. We were all tired and feeling terrible over the losses we had suffered. We were quartered in a house and thought we would be able to sleep that night -- the 406th had gone through us so there was no danger of a frontal attack. Bilyk and I had been given up as dead, so the fellows were glad to see us.

John Skene, 405-F

Finally, the time for the assault came, and we moved up in the dark, somewhere between Lenox and Worsdorf. It was obvious the Germans had zeroed in on the potential crossing points, because as we approached the river, we could hear the mortars dropping right in what had to be the area where people were attempting to make crossings ahead of us. There was a steep road down to the area near the river. Engineers had boats ready. There were about 15-16 of us in a boat. I remember thinking to myself that this was too many people for this size boat in the type of river we were trying to cross, where the current was so swift. I also had a lot of sympathy for the engineers who had been down there for a considerable period of time, getting others ahead of us across. And just before we got to the river, another barrage of mortars landed right in middle of the stream. We managed to get into the boat, get it into the river, and start across with the paddles. Most of the people in the boat had laid their Mae West life preservers in the bottom of the boat. We got across the river; and hit the bank on the other side, but the bank was above the head of the man in the front of the boat, and the boat hit it, dropped back a little bit, spun, and suddenly capsized. The river was moving very rapidly, and was icy cold. I remember thinking to myself, here I've been swimming all of my life, considered myself to be a better than average swimmer, and in all likelihood I was going to drown. All of us were carrying extra bandoliers of ammunition, and satchels for the bazooka ammunition, and whatever extra supplies we could. These were to be dropped on the opposite bank for the troops following us to pick up, or to be used as reserve supplies. It was totally confusing, the first moment in the water. My helmet was gone quickly, and I was struggling to get the bandoliers of bazooka and rifle ammunition off of my shoulders. The water was over my head and I kept going down and bouncing off the bottom and coming up to get a breath, all the time working to get this stuff off my back. On coming up one time, I saw one of the Mae West life preservers floating by and grabbed it with one arm, which I had free. I was then able to get the rest of the stuff off my back, my packsack, with my new hunting knife and all was swept off and down the river. By this time, one of the members of my platoon started floating by. He was in bad shape. It was a fellow named Thompson. I grabbed him and pulled him onto the preserver with me. I had no idea how far down the river we'd been swept. I wondered at the time whether the Germans occupied the bank on their side, and whether we had any forces on the bank on our side, because if we were able to get to shore, we would prefer to come out on the American side of the river. Its a good thing this assault was done in the dark, because the Germans could have picked off many people that were floating down that river. Finally, we came to a point where the river curved, and there was a pile of brush on the American side that jutted out into the river. We managed to grab hold of this. I held on to Thompson and the preserver, and found another fellow had already washed up on this, and he was able to help me get Thompson out of the river and up on to this bunch of brush. It turned out he was one of the engineers that had been working on the crossing, and going back and forth across the river for some reason. The three of us made it to the shoreline, and headed upstream, where we had fallen into the river. In route, we could hear the mortars up ahead falling in on the troops that were still trying to get across. We were walking along the bank, and I heard calls from the river. Looking out, I found two fellows who were within 5 or 10 feet of the bank. With some branches and whatnot, we were able to get them out of the river also. I don't know what happened to Thompson, after we got to shore. I thought he was with me, but he had disappeared. Later ran into him up at the aid station. We followed the river back up to what was then the town of Lenox, which meant we'd come quite a ways downstream in that current, and we were directed toward an aid station, where they were taking in the wounded and those who had fallen into the river, and issuing dry clothes, and in general fixing them up. I ran into a couple members of our squad in this rest area. Frank Radke was one. I don't recall offhand who the others were. We took stock at that point and of those who had gotten on that little boat, he and I and Bill Tideback, possibly Al Hawton, were the only ones we knew who had gotten out of the boat. I don't know whether the ones who were missing were killed by enemy fire or drowned in the river. Our history book says there were no drownings, but I seriously doubt that. At any rate, John Stivali was missing, Bob Dryer was missing, Bill White was missing but we later found he was a prisoner. Bill Veet was missing, but he was also, we heard, taken prisoner. Jack Sloan was missing. And there was one other fellow who I have a picture of in my scrapbook. I cannot recall his name. He was missing. We exchanged tales while we were in this aid station. As time went on, someone came in finally, and started making efforts to organize the groups so they could rejoin their units. They outfitted us with dry clothes and new weapons and equipment. We also had a hot meal, and then got together with others and headed for the front lines. I don't recall much about the fighting that ensued when we rejoined our units, but I do remember that a German counter -- attack with tanks gave the 3rd battalion of our regiment a pretty bad time in and around Bosler. After the activity in our sector died down, we had a little time. We had noticed four American tanks not too far in from our positions. So, Bill Tideback and I went over to take a look at them. Each had a small hole, obviously made by the German 88mm gun, which was bad news for tanks. I looked into one of them, and it was awful, what it had done to the interior of that tank, and the people in the tank. But all we got out of that little adventure was a new respect for the German 88mm gun, and -- a case of C rations which we found on one of the burned out tanks.

Jim Hansen, 405-F

I don't recall which squad I was supposed to cross with. We reached the edge of the water and slid the nose of the boat into the water, jumped in and did just as we were taught in the training sessions. To help our crossing, the artillery loaded smoke-shells and we couldn't see the other riverbank. The river was very swift and the boats were impossible to guide. We whirled around and around and what seemed like 15 minutes we hit the shore, an we jumped out to hold the boat while the rest scrambled out. I said, "Lets get away from this Da--- river," and we really got a move on. As I ran I spotted some building that looked like the objective of the 1st platoon. We fanned out in a fighting formation and started to move out. One of the men called out, "Hey Sgt., we better get back to the river. I think the rest are retreating." The smoke cleared a little and we saw more GIs carrying boats down to the river. I replyed, "HELL, were on the same side of the river we started out from." Back to the Roer we ran, grabbed a boat and jumped in. The current grabbed the boat and tore it out of the grasp of the men. Not wanting to be an admiral without a crew I bailed out. Luckily as the boat hit the shore again, I jumped, and we went back to get another boat. As the smoke cleared we paddled like hell and got to the other shore. By this time the engineers had a cable on the other side. It almost swamped us, but we were across this time.

As we moved away from the river I found another of the 1st platoon squads and a squad of the 2nd Platoon. There was no sign of Junior or the other squads. We headed for the 1st platoon objective hoping to find Jr. on the way. The smoke cleared and all we could see were German land mines. I halted everyone and got them in a single file and told them to step only in my shoe tracks. I was not that brave, but got caught in front and it would have been hard to order out scouts at that time. After what seemed like hours, we passed thru the minefield. I held my breath as the last man cleared the field. I now turned my attention to the buildings, which I could see more clearly. I saw two Germans looking at us from a clump of trees I again spread the men out in fighting formation and laid down fire on the woods and we moved on at a run. We had quite a fire fight. The BARs jammed and a German was only 20 feet from me. His rifle was on the other side of the tree and couldn't fire on me. As he started to raise his rifle, Sgt. Smith blasted him. I owe him my life. The shooting stopped and there was not one live German in sight. I was amazed that they could disappear so fast. I ordered my men to hit the dirt and lie quiet for a while. Soon a white flag came up from a hole. Then the head of a German soldier.

These pictures were taken by Pfc Larry Darcy from McKee's Rocks, Pennsylvania, who haunted the riverbank as soon as daylight broke on the morning of 23 February, the day of the big push across the Roer. This photo shows troops crossing under artillery and mortar fire, carrying ammunition to bridgehead forces.

Assault boats piled against debris by the furious currents, which swept out two support bridges.

On a Roer River footbridge lies the body of an American soldier who was hit by German mortar-shell fragments when he was only 50 feet from east bank. (this was the first photograph approved by military censors in WWII for distribution that showed a dead American GI)

The Roer River crossing was among the bloodiest American campaigns in Europe, and it was here Digger was wounded on 23 February. Five and a half decades after Digger's death his wife Helen told me her, Digger, and young Sue Ellen attended a 102nd Infantry Division reunion, and a man approached them and said to Digger, "if you hadn't been in our boat during that crossing we all would have drowned" Apparently, Digger was in one of the leading assault waves and all those years he spent on the water piloting a fishing boat proved useful.

According to the Division history, the 1st Battalion was the assault wave at Rurdorf, and because of the narrowness of the regimental front, only one Company could cross at a time. The second Battalion, including F Company, crossed under fire in boats about one hour after the initial assault began. Once across, Companies F and G advanced abreast and succeeded in capturing the high ground east of Tetz by 0930.

With the 102nd Infantry Division Through Germany:

"The Roer crossing was the most vital and exacting operation of the entire war for the 102nd Division. In the furious and confusing actions many men emerged as heroes. Others fought in obscurity and anonymity, but their efforts were not in vain."

The Distinguished Service Cross is the nation's second highest medal for valor, exceeded only by the Medal of Honor. That three such prestigious awards were earned by troops of the 405th during the Roer River crossing is a testament to the challenges encountered and overcome during the operation. Lt. James L. Hansen (*Jim Hansen, 405-F),* whose initial river crossing attempt landed him and his boat on the same shore from which they departed, was one of the recipients of the DSC that day. The citation for the award reads:

After crossing the river, Company F, 405th Infantry, was scattered by heavy enemy barrages. Lt. James L. Hansen, leader of the 1st Platoon, reorganized his unit, personally sought out and killed the enemy manning a machine-gun emplacement that impeded his company's advance and then led a furious, well-conceived attack. Through his courage and outstanding leadership, he was largely responsible for the success of his unit in seizing its objective.

The outstanding accomplishments of the 405th Infantry Regiment during the Roer River campaign were recognized in the form of a Presidential Unit Citation. The requirements for receiving this award are described below.

Criteria: The Presidential Unit Citation is awarded to units of the Armed Forces of the United States and co-belligerent nations for extraordinary heroism in action against an armed enemy occurring on or after 7 December 1941. The unit must display such gallantry, determination, and esprit de corps in accomplishing its mission under extremely difficult and hazardous conditions as to set it apart and above other units participating in the same campaign. The degree of heroism required is the same as that which would warrant award of a Distinguished Service Cross to an individual. Extended periods of combat duty or participation in a large number of operational missions, either ground or air is not sufficient. This award will normally be earned by units that have participated in single or successive actions covering relatively brief time spans. It is not reasonable to presume that entire units can sustain Distinguished Service Cross performance for extended time periods except under the most unusual circumstances. Only on rare occasions will a unit larger than battalion qualify for award of this decoration.

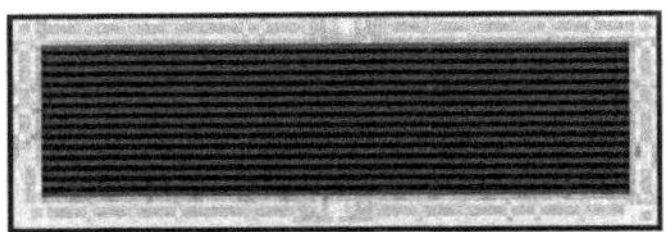
Presidential Unit Citation

GENERAL ORDERS WAR DEPARTMENT
No. 16 Washington 25, D.C., 5 February 1947
* * *
BATTLE HONORS.— As authorized by Executive Order 9396 (sec. I, WD Bul. 22, 1943); superseding Executive Order 9075 (sec. III, WD Bul. II, 1942), the following units are cited by the War Department under the provisions of section IV, WD Circular 333, 1943, in the name of the President of the United States as public evidence of deserved honor and distinction. The citation reads as follows:
* * *
The *405th Infantry Regiment* and the following supporting units:

1276th Engineer Combat Battalion;
Company A, 327th Engineer Combat Battalion;
Company B, (less one platoon), 327th Engineer Combat Battalion;
Forward Observation Parties, 379th Field Artillery Battalion;
Forward Observation Parties, Company A, 3d Chemical Mortar Battalion,

are cited for outstanding performance of duty in action on 23 and 24 February 1945, during the crossing of the Roer River at Rurdorf, Germany and the establishment of a bridgehead in that vicinity. With only two possible crossing sites in the sector, one of which was rendered useless by the destruction of a dam and the resulting inundation of large portions of the river valley, the regiment was forced to cross in column of companies on a one-company front. When leading elements started crossing in assault boats at 0330, 23 February 1945, the enemy reacted quickly and laid down a terrific barrage on the single crossing site. Braving this deadly hail of fire and struggling against..... the treacherous current of the flooded river, the regiment succeeded in crossing by sheer courage and determination. Despite the loss of men and equipment in the icy waters, units were assembled quickly on the far bank and started for their objectives. Traversing over 2,000 yards of flat, soggy, partially inundated river valley, overrunning and capturing, frequently by hand-to-hand combat, a maze of strongly defended emplacements and trenches, passing through numerous mine fields and barbed wire entanglements, and constantly under direct fire and observation from the escarpment beyond, assault elements succeeded in capturing the town of Tetz and the high ground beyond the river valley. Beating off a strong counterattack, the regiment continued its attack, driving through the Tetz-Boslar Valley and capturing the town of Boslar and the high ground to the northwest. Unable to proceed beyond Boslar because of withering fire from enemy tanks and infantry on the high ground to the northeast, the regiment dug in, with orders to hold at all costs-pending the arrival of tanks, tank destroyers, antitank guns, and other supporting weapons, which had been unable to cross the river. Quickly launching a counterattack against Boslar, the enemy succeeded in penetrating the forward positions, but, after a vicious fight, was forced to withdraw. Later, another attack was launched against Boslar, but was stopped before it reached the town. Still later, a third attack was launched against the same sector, which was led by some 30 tanks and self-propelled guns, followed closely by about 200 infantrymen. Striking with great force, the enemy quickly overran forward positions and penetrated as far as the battalion reserve line. Forward elements and company support, refusing to yield an inch of ground, allowed themselves to be overrun and then emerged from their positions to engage enemy infantry from the front, flanks, and rear. Fierce fighting raged throughout the town. Calling for artillery fire to be laid on their own positions, the defenders finally succeeded in clearing the town and forcing the enemy to withdraw. The enemy launched four additional attacks against Boslar during the night. Three were thrown back before reaching the town and the fourth, although penetrating it slightly, was finally repulsed by the same relentless, unwavering determination and repeated individual feats of heroism which characterized the entire action. Throughout the remainder of the regimental sector, the enemy launched numerous smaller counterattacks during the night, but all were thrown back with heavy losses. By dawn, all positions were completely restored and intact. Despite continuous and savage fighting without rest or respite for over 27 hours, members of the regiment climaxed a brilliant initial success by jumping off at dawn in continuation of the attack, which never once failed to capture a single objective. The conspicuous gallantry, esprit de corps, indomitable fighting spirit and determination displayed by the members of the *405th Infantry Regiment* and its supporting units are in keeping with the highest traditions of the United States Army.

* * *

ORDER OF THE SECRETARY OF *WAR:*

G. C. MARSHALL
Chief of Staff

OFFICIAL: EDWARD F. WITSELL
Major General
Acting Adjutant General

From an article in LIFE magazine, March 12, 1945:

Since December the U. S. First and Ninth Armies had been building up strength behind the swollen little Roer River. On Feb.23 they let it go with a stunning night barrage. The Germans at the river were quickly overpowered. Beyond the river, the rigid framework of their Rhineland defense began to break down. A week after the first gun had been fired at the Roer, the Ninth had arrived at the Rhine opposite Dusseldorf. The men of the Ninth exchanged shots with the Germans on the other side.

Greenberg 405-F

Thursday, February 25.

We spent the day resting and reorganizing. There weren't many of us left so two squads were formed out of what was formerly three and this included the four new replacements that arrived in the morning. E company was nearby, and I was happy to learn that Aaron was fine. We heard that the 405th and the 406th reg't had taken their objectives and that we were soon to move up again. We also learned that the American armored forces were about to cross the river to give us some support, which we didn't mind at all.

Greenberg 405-F
Friday, February 26.

In the morning, we moved forward. We walked about 4 miles to Boslar where we were told we would spend the day. Five minutes later we were told we would move to Hottorf which was in the process of being taken. As we approached the town, we could count 15 American tanks knocked out, plus many of the tank men dead. This town wasn't a pushover. We relieved the outfit that had taken the town and remained in the trenches. When night approached, we dug new foxholes and when we were finished we fired tracers into the many haystacks that were in front of us, putting them on fire. This would disclose any Jerry's hiding in them and it kept the area in front of us lit all night. The company suffered a few casualties during the night.

The next major objective for the U.S. Army was to capture the area between the Roer River and the west bank of the Rhine River. Berlin may have been Germany's capital, but the area between the Roer and the Rhine, known as the Cologne plain, was in 1945, Germany's industrial heartland. The Rhine, which is the major river in Germany, begins near Andermatt Switzerland and travels northward through Germany until it finally empties into the North Sea south of Rotterdam in the Netherlands.

Beginning on February 24, the Ozarks attacked northwest from Rurdorf towards the city of Duisburg on the Rhine. The distance was only about 39 miles, but there were many towns both large and small that had to be pacified along the way. The major battles for the 102nd on the path to the Rhine were for Munchen-

Gladbach, then Krefeld, Uerdingen, and Rheinhausen, which sat on the west bank of the Rhine. During the Rhine River offensive Digger was awarded the Bronze Star medal, but because of the post war loss of military records no citation is available for either this decoration or Digger's Purple Heart.

The 102nd Division history states:

"*We did not know that the soft mud, open terrain, and many dug-in enemy 88s would slow, and eventually bog down our and supporting armor. The tanks of the 701st Tank Battalion were badly in need of servicing. They had done a superior job but had taken a terrific beating. The crews were tired and weary and had not slept for days.*"

Army Regulation 600-8-22 (Military Awards)

Bronze Star Medal

a. The Bronze Star Medal was established by Executive Order 9419, 4 February 1944 (superseded by Executive Order 11046, 24 August 1962).

b. The Bronze Star Medal is awarded to any person who, while serving in any capacity in or with the Army of the United States after 6 December 1941, distinguished himself or herself by heroic or meritorious achievement or service, not involving participation in aerial flight, in connection with military operations against an armed enemy; or while engaged in military operations involving conflict with an opposing armed force in which the United States is not a belligerent party.

c. Awards may be made for acts of heroism, performed under circumstances described above, which are of lesser degree than required for the award of the Silver Star.

The German opposition between the Roer and the Rhine consisted of a mixture of good soldiers in their 20s, boys of 15 and 16, railroad battalions, Volkssturmer, and Air Force ground personnel. On the whole, they were far from first-rate troops. Hitler had gambled 500,000 troops during the battle of the Bulge. Of these, 100,000 troops were killed, wounded or captured, and eight hundred tanks were destroyed. As a result of German losses in the Ardennes, and the unexpectedly rapid Allied drive eastward from the Roer, the defenses encountered were not as formidable as those previously confronted.

102nd Division history:

Few deliberate defensive installations were encountered between Viersen and the Rhine. Old antiaircraft emplacements, parts of the Ruhr perimeter defense system, were troublesome. Antitank obstacles were not formidable, being scorned even by the local inhabitants who dubbed them "one hour-one-minute obstacles" because, as the Germans said, "the American tankers laugh for one hour, tear them down in one minute."

At the same time a new method of aircraft identification was gaining popularity among the Nazi troops. This method was the essence of simplicity, running something like this: "If the planes are dark colored, they're British. If the planes are light colored, they're American. If the planes are invisible- that's the Luftwaffe!"

Dick Skene, 405-F

The assault across the Roer had the Germans on the run. Our commanders didn't give us much breathing room either. They had us hot on their trail, following the armored forces, and in some cases, bypassing pockets of Germans to be mopped up by those behind us. I remember going across fields, coming to a farmhouse, keeping our weapons aimed at the farmhouse, shooting out all the windows as we passed by. And, at one farmhouse we stopped because we had sensed that there were some people there. We found a large number of people in the basement, mostly civilians. Any prisoners that were taken were immediately shuffled off to the rear. I remember we spent a little time in one of these places where a large number of the Germans finally came out of the cellars to surrender. And, after we had disposed of these people, handed them over to other people to take back to the rear, we were rushed off out into the open again, and at this time I was in the wrong positon in our squad. I was where Oscar Boostos should have been, and he was where I should have been. I remember seeing a shell, it could have been a mortar shell, land almost at Oscar's feet and explode. Bobby Gonzales, the medic who was attached to us, ran over to Oscar, just for a minute. Then, he took the rifle, stuck it in the ground, hanging his helmet on it, and came back over to join us. Everything was pretty disorganized. The point from where the mortar shell had been fired was off on our right, and the direction that we were moving, we were going to bypass the Germans that were in that general area. The days ran into each other as we moved across to the Rhine River. We were either on the move, sometime following tanks, which wasn't my favorite occupation, but other times resting in houses. We seldom dug holes unless we were caught in the open. I recall seeing a little bit of the German Luftwaffe at this point and actually watched from the ground a couple of dogfights that the Germans had with our aircraft. I remember one American or British aircraft that had been damaged in a dogfight, that flew back over our lines, with a German hot on his tail. By the time he got there, he realized he was over the wrong troops. Everybody was shooting at him, with machine guns, rifles, whatever. He turned around and took off. The American plane was not running very well but he managed to go behind our lines if he had to come down.

Greenberg 405-F

Monday, March 1.

At midnight we were relieved and walked back to a town 3 miles away for a rest. I started carrying a portable typewriter, passed it on to the other fellows, got tired of carrying it and threw it away. Brophy was here to join us. He had lost his glasses in the Roer River and went back for new ones. We ate at 2 A.M., slept till 4 A.M. when we were awakened and told we were to attack again. We walked about 2 hours and then attacked. We didn't have much trouble till we were near the town we were to take. Suddenly a German -- Tiger Tank started firing from beside a house directly in front of us. We were on flat ground with no protection. Munger was killed instantly on the first burst. I saw a 1 ft. trench and made a dash for it. Some of the other fellows did the same. We were still in a dangerous position as the tank could rake the trench. Luckily Yank artillery came to our aid and the Tiger tank took off. We entered the town, rested for an hour, and reformed to attack again.

We attacked, took the Munchen-Gladback airport and dug in. We saw two Jerry tanks moving in front of us, but we couldn't do anything with rifles. During these attacks we had only a little support from our armor because they were stopped by anti -- tank ditches surrounding all these towns. We were relieved and returned to the town we had captured in the morning.

In the morning, I was in the latrine in a compromising position when suddenly looked up to see an air battle over my head. I hurriedly finished what I was doing and went to the safety of the house as shrapnel of ack-ack was falling. However the sky was filled with American and German planes. It was a complete victory for the Americans. Five Jerry planes were shot down by our P-47s -- three in flames. We did not lose any. We then marched four miles and attacked another town. However, we took it without firing a shot. The 5th Armored to our amazement had already taken it. We had some excitement when a fellow found three Jerry's in a cellar. From the way they were dressed we thought they were the German Generalstaff. They turned out to be the Chief of Police, Fire, and Sanitation, but from our Colonel down we thought we had Hitler's advisors.

Greenberg 405-F

Wednesday, March 3.

In the morning, we walked seven miles to attack Krefeld, detouring at one point to capture another town without trouble. As the whole division, plus the 84th division and the 5th armored maneuvered to take Krefeld, which is a large city, F company was in battalion reserve but still up in the attack. As we approached German firing became terrific. Suddenl,y out of nowhere, came a blinding snowstorm which blotted out everything in front of us. I and two other fellows were told to take back about 100 Jerry prisoners that the company in front of us captured. We took them to an anti -- tank ditch a little behind and searched them. We then took them back to the M.P.s and since it was dark and we didn't know where the company was, we spent the night with the M.P.s.

Greenberg 405-F
Thursday, March 4.

In the morning, we went into Krefeld to rejoin the company. Jerry had retreated during the night leaving us the whole place. We learned that the 102nd division had been placed in the 9th army reserve, so that meant we were going to get a good rest. On rejoining the company, we learned that we were going to another part of the town to get quarters to live in. When we got there, we found that it was a pretty good deal. Each platoon had a small apartment building to himself. There were plenty of beds, places to wash and take a bath, which was a treat for us.

2nd Battalion HW at Krefeld. (Digger)

DPs, (displaced persons) who were forced to work in the Krefeld steel mill, celebrate their liberation.

First Jewish synagogue re-opens in Krefeld.

Greenberg 405-F

Friday, March 5.

We started to get settled in our new quarters and we also started to explore the town. Krefeld is a large city, and this was the first experience we had had with a great number of civilians. We walked around always with our rifles, and the people were actually afraid of us. They had been fed the type of propaganda that made them imagine we would kill all of them first chance we had. Krefeld had been bombed only twice by our bombers, but large areas of the city was in ruins showing that the bombings were not light. We also learned that the 84th division was also quartered in this town.

L to R: Edwin Harwell, Redus Moran, William Rivers, Kenneth Walker, John J. Burke, Ertis Milam, Ray Nider. Don't know the fellow in the door. (Digger)

L to R: Rivers (kitchen), Harwell (kitchen), Blake (supply), Walker (kitchen). (Digger)

Greenberg 405-F

Saturday, March 13.

This evening, we had quite a show. We were in the house and about 10 P.M. we heard some heavy gunfire. We ran outside and looking toward the river we could see bright flashes where Allied bombers were dropping their loads on a German city on the other side of the Rhine. It was a very heavy raid and there was plenty of enemy ack-ack fire. Occasionally in the distance we could see a plane burst into flames and plunge to the ground. On one occasion, some German night fighters hit a four-engine bomber, which burst into flames right above us. We saw some parachutes open in the dim light and the big bomber crashed quite near us. The whine of a crashing plane is the most eerie sound I think there is.

We were all called together in the morning by the C.O. and told we were going on a secret mission the next day. He said he couldn't give us any information except that it wasn't going to be a dangerous mission and we might actually enjoy it. He told us it was so secret that the brass higher up in the reg't and division did not know about it. We were told to pack our belongings and to remove the 102nd div. shoulder patch. All the trucks removed their unit numbers. We were also told that the whole battalion would be going on the mission with us. The men speculated and were a bit excited -- their speculation ranged from guarding a peace conference to going somewhere to Russia.

Greenberg 405-F

Monday, March 15.

In the morning, we loaded up on trucks and took off. We figured we wouldn't be gone too long as we left behind a few men to guard the house. After traveling about 20 miles we were surprised to learn we had reached our destination. The C.O. called us together and then we learned what our job was going to be. We were going to be Co. F of the 314th reg't of the 79th div. We were to sew the 79th div. patch on our shoulder and the trucks were to put 79th div. unit numbers on. It seemed that the real Co. F. of the 79th had shipped off during the night to the Rhine River in preparation for crossing the river. It seemed the Germans were sending radio messages across the river saying what units were where and what they were doing. The deception was to make the Germans think that the 79th div. was still back and not getting ready to cross the river. To enlighten the deception all the companies guarded about 10 miles of woods in which there was every kind of equipment available including planes, trucks, tanks, and guns. The funny part of it was that all this equipment was dummies -- rubber balloons filled up. We had guards posted all over keeping German civilians out and thus giving the Germans the idea that there was something pretty important in those woods. It must have worked because at night German planes would come over the woods dropping flares to see what they could see. During the day we would ride around in trucks all over the countryside to let the people see to what outfit we belonged. The Germans never did catch on to what happened even when the 79th made a successful crossing of the river. The secret was well kept till the end of the war.

Greenberg 405-F
Friday, March 19.

From where we sat on guard, we could see the road that led up to the Rhine. All day long the roads were clogged with supplies being brought up in anticipation of the Rhine crossing. Tanks, boats of the U.S. Navy, large guns, etc. It looked like this crossing was to be the final blow on the Germans. During the day large fleets of American bombers flew overhead. It was a beautiful sight for us, but I imagine not for others. We could see clouds of tinfoil being dropped from the planes. The reason for this was to jam German radar from picking up the American planes.

It was during late March of 1945, that the U.S. Third Army under Gen. Patton began its famous bridging and crossing operations of the Rhine. After the completion of the Battle in the Ardennes, Patton and his Army turned to the south and east, attacking toward the Rhine. Without the luck of the 9th Armored Division, further to the north, who were able to capture the only intact bridge across the Rhine at Remagen, Patton's Third Army faced the necessity of bridging the wide river with their own resources. There had been a total of twenty-two road and 25 railroad bridges spanning the Rhine in Germany, but with the exception of the Remagen Bridge, they had all been destroyed.

Greenberg 405-F
Tuesday, March 23.

Now that the Allies had crossed the Rhine River there was no reason for us to stay here so we were not surprised when we were told to get our stuff together and be ready to move the next day.

One thing it was necessary for us to know was the password. This was the password that was the same all over the front and it was changed every 24 hours starting at noon. It was necessary for us to remember it cause it was most embarrassing to be halted in the dark by a Yank soldier and be asked the password and not know it as a bullet might follow. Of course, this worked both ways, cause if we heard someone approaching without the password we used our rifles.

Digger, Sam Paul-Jeep driver, Gonzales-medic (Digger)

The Ozark Division was relieved of the responsibility for the defense of the Rhine River in early April, and boarded some 1,750 vehicles, and began its journey to cross the river at Wessel. The Karnes' family history incorrectly states: "*In the war, Digger served in the European Theater of Operations. The most notable operation he was involved with was the crossing of the Rhine at the bridge at Remagen. He may have received a purple heart during that operation.*"

Greenberg 405-F
Wednesday, April 7.

At about 1 A.M. we boarded very large trucks and trailers. As we went north and approached the Wessel bridgehead all the trucks started putting on their headlights. This was quite a surprise to us as this was the first time we had ever seen Yank trucks up near the front with their headlights on. The traffic was quite heavy as we came closer and we hoped that no Jerry plane was nearby. When we came near the bridge head, we saw a sight we hardly expected. There were two pontoon bridges crossing the river - traffic going only one way - toward the Germans. Although it was night the whole area was lit up as if it were daylight. Anti-aircraft were all over the place on the alert. In the sky we could dimly see barrage balloons, which were for the purpose of preventing Jerry dive bombers from destroying the bridges.

Digger and someone unknown. (Digger)

(Digger) bottom left

Greenberg 405-F

Friday, April 9.

In the morning, we climbed in our trucks and advanced about another 40 miles. It seemed that German opposition was melting away. We spent part of the day cleaning up the town but after that was finished we did other things. We collected chickens and pigs and prepared them so we could eat. Coolidge came around in a Weasel, and I jumped in it with him and went off into the country and collected about four dozen eggs for the fellows. Some, or rather most of the fellows went around looking for something to drink and they were quite successful most of the time. In a short period of time, most of the fellows were drunk or sick and having one hell of a time. However, no one was hungry because of the chickens, pigs, eggs, potatoes, and cognac.

Front row: Milam, Walker, Harwell, Moran
Back row: Karnes, Hartz, Burke (Digger)

With the 102nd Infantry Division Through Germany

The Germans were faced by reverses on all fronts. In the west, the situation for the enemy had never been so grave. Hitler had either underestimated the Allied strength, refusing that we were capable of striking into and beyond the center of Germany, or he was deliberately allowing Western Germany to fall into Allied hands. Radio Berlin still droned about 'shortening lines, inflicting tremendous losses,' carrying on the momentum of earlier propaganda policies. There was yet no indication of national surrender, although individual surrender increased every day. The only apparent strategy was to delay, delay for what purpose, no one, not even the German High Command itself, was sure.

On 12 April, XIII Corps attacked from Hanover toward the Elbe

River. The 102nd Division moved out on the right, following the 5th Armored Division spearhead, and maintained contact with the 84th on the left and 35th Infantry Division on the right.

In the four-day dash from the Leine to the Elbe River no great resistance was expected, nor encountered. Without reserves, without transport, without food and often without ammunition, knowing their rear areas were in the hands of our armor, the enemy had little choice but to surrender. In the woods, movements were partly screened and those who no longer wanted to fight could at least hide. Stragglers and malingerers continued to be flushed out of these areas until the end of the month. For the most part, however, the enemy either withdrew to the north, and eventually crossed the river, or he gave up. The chief danger lay in by-passed units that cannot always be tracked down in the neat forests. Every patch of woods became a potential ambush. Unescorted vehicles and small detachments therefore sometimes ran into difficulties. But the Germans had little taste and less talent for guerrilla warfare, nor did the sullen and melancholy populace give them the support which is necessary for a real success in this kind of fighting.

Greenberg 405-F
Monday, April 12.

We found out in the morning why we hadn't chased Jerry late last night. A surrender had been arranged for this morning at Gardelegen, a town about 30 miles away. A Jerry regiment was to formally surrender to our regiment. We boarded our trucks and took off to Gardelegen being on the alert and taking every precaution against a German trick. When we arrived, the German regt. was lined up and proceeded to pile up their weapons and ammo. After this was done we found some pretty good quarters and made ourselves comfortable as we expected to stay here awhile. We were only a few miles from the Elbe and it seemed the war was bout over for us.

John Skene, 405-F

I do recall another incident. We were walking through the woods to clean out Germans that might be occupying the woods, and we ran across a large number of escaped concentration camp people. They were in the typical striped uniforms. They were pitiful. They were starving to death. Some had apparently gotten away and been hiding in the woods, attempting to obtain food when they could. But they were a pitiful bunch, and we gave them what K rations we had, and they would get down on the ground and kiss your feet. I don't know whether they were all Jewish, but they spoke more than one language. I suspect that a lot of them were Polish; some may have been Russians, or Jews from other parts of Europe.

Greenberg 405-F

Tuesday, April 13.

It was while taking a walk with Racine and DiGiovanni that I came across the most horrible sight I had ever seen. We stopped to talk to a Polish woman for a minute, and she pointed out a very large shed and told us to look in it. We went toward this building and on going into it we saw a sight that we would never forget. Inside the building were hundreds of bodies that were smoking. Later we learned the whole story. It seemed the night before we entered Gaidelegen, SS troops took 1200 prisoners and put them inside this shed. The shed was filled with straw and all entrances were guarded with machine guns and bazookas. The Germans then proceeded to machine gun the men in cold blood. In the confusion that followed, two prisoners escaped and that's how the story finally came out. When the Germans thought they killed everyone they poured gasoline on the bodies and lit it. While looking on this scene we heard a moan and found one man still alive. We called the medics and he was taken to the hospital but died the next morning. Within the next week all the Germans in the town were forced to pick up the bodies and dig graves for them. It wasn't pleasant work, but Jerry was still getting off too easy. Gardelegen proved to any skeptic in the division that German atrocities were true.

More than a thousand people, most of whom were Poles, were burned alive or shot trying to escape. They were slave laborers evacuated from the Mittelbau-Dora and Hannover-Stocken concentration camps, who were removed from a transportation train, herded into the barn, and summarily massacred.

With the 102nd Infantry Division Through Germany

The surrender of Gardelegen climaxed the Elbe campaign. This victory has a tragic conclusion, however, the first indications of which were discovered by members of the 2nd Battalion, 405th, who were engaged in a routine search of the area surrounding the Luftwaffe airfield. At the top of a knoll overlooking the airfield and the city, our troops found a large masonry hay-storage shed, typical of the Altmark countryside. Several prison uniformed bodies, riddled with bullet wounds and peculiarly charred, lay twisted in the green spring wheat nearby. Reconnoitering the exterior, the men saw five more bodies sprawled through a jagged hole in the masonry. Finally, when one of the great wooden doors was pushed open there issued forth to pollute the early spring morning, a cloud of smoke and the stench of burned flesh. Overcoming their nausea, the soldiers explored the forbidding interior to find heaped there in contortions characteristic of the most violent agonies of death the charred and smoking bodies of what they estimated to be at least three hundred men. Here Poles, Frenchmen, Dutchmen, Belgians, an American, and even Germans had been deliberately burned alive.

An investigation later disclosed that 1,016 political and military prisoners had perished in this building. Seven prisoners escaped from the barn. The massacre at Gaidelegen occurred on April 13, 1945, less than a month before the end of WWII in Europe. The following excerpts from the *Holocaust Encyclopedia* describe the events at Gaidelegen:

"On the afternoon of April 13, 100 SS, Luftwaffe, and labor front soldiers forced the 1,100 remaining prisoners inside a barn. SS troops spread gasoline on the straw-covered floor and locked the prisoners inside. For the rest of the night, the troops threw hand grenades, shot flares, and fired bullets into the barn, burning it to the ground. Two days later, American troops found charred remains and fewer than 20 prisoners left alive."

By April 19, 1945, the story of the Gardelegen massacre began appearing in the western press. On that day, both the *New York Times* and *The Washington Post* ran stories on the massacre, quoting one American soldier who stated: *"I never was so sure before of exactly what I was fighting for. Before this you would have said those stories were propaganda, but now you know they weren't. There are the bodies and all those guys are dead."*

Photos show American troops at the Gardelegen barn after it burned
Photo credit: US Holocaust Memorial Museum

Fully clothed bodies were exhumed from mass grave near barn, shown on the left.

The description on the back of the photo reads: Gardelegen
1300 dead in this barn. (Digger)

On April 21, 1945, the local commander of the 102nd ordered between 200 and 300 men from the town of Gardelegen to give the murdered prisoners a proper burial. Over the next few days, the German civilians exhumed 586 bodies from the trenches, and recovered 430 bodies from the barn, placing each in an individual grave. On April 25, the Ozark Division held a ceremony to honor the dead, and erected a memorial tablet to the victims, which stated that the townspeople of Gardelegen are charged with the responsibility that the "graves are forever kept as green as the memory of these unfortunates will be kept in the hearts of freedom-loving men everywhere."

Also on April 25, Colonel George Lynch addressed German civilians at Gardelegen with the following statement:

The German people have been told that stories of German atrocities were Allied propaganda. Here, you can see for yourself. Some will say that the Nazis were responsible for this crime. Others will point to the Gestapo. The responsibility rests with neither -- it is the responsibility of the German people....Your so-called Master Race has demonstrated that it is master only of crime, cruelty and sadism. You have lost the respect of the civilized world.

Gerhard Thiele

According to the book entitled "Die Todesmärche and das Massaker von Gardelegen," by Diana Gring, the man who gave the order to kill the prisoners, Gerhard Thiele, escaped on April 14th by disguising himself in the uniform of a German soldier, and traveling with false papers. Thiele lived in the Western zone of occupation, and later in West Germany, under a fake identity. His wife continued to live in East Germany and never revealed his whereabouts. Thiele died in 1994 at the age of eighty-five, a fugitive from justice who was never tried for the war crimes he perpetrated upon innocent civilians.

Gardelegen was in the province of Sachsen-Anhalt, which became part of the Soviet zone of occupation. On July 1, 1945, the province was turned over to the Soviet Union under a prior Allied agreement. Although the American military had jurisdiction over the Gardelegen war criminals by virtue of the fact that American troops had liberated Nordhausen-Dora, the concentration camp from which the prisoners had been transported to Gardelegen, the American military turned the matter over to the Soviet Union for prosecution. On July 25, 1946, the twenty-one men who were accused in the Gardelegen massacre were handed over to the Soviet Union along with all the evidence and documentation on the case. These twenty-one men were brought before a Soviet Military Tribunal, and after being convicted, were sentenced to long prison terms in one of the "special camps" set up by the Soviets in Communist East Germany.

John Skene, 405-F

After the events of Garlegen, we moved on up to the large city of Stendal on the Elb River. At this point, it was our general understanding that this was as far as we were going to go, although one of the companies of the 102nd Division had crossed the river and proceeded a few miles, almost to within the outskirts of Berlin, but had to turn around and come back. It seems it was at this point that our politicians at home, along with the agreements made with the Russians, had decided what course the war was going to take. In essence, we were instructed we could not accept the surrender of the Germans who were being heavily beaten by the Russians on the other front. And the Russians, by this time were in Berlin. I recall, however, that in spite of these instructions that there were large numbers of Germans who were marching down the streets of Stendal, and piling their weapons into large stacks as instructed, and headed for prisoner of war status. But we were placed in some of the small towns around the outskirts of Stendal, fairly close to the Elb River to await the arrival of the Russians.

Stendal (Digger)

Heinie plane in the woods at Stendal (Digger)
(This aircraft appears to be a Focke-Wulf 190 fighter)

Heinie plane in the woods close to airfield at Stendal. It was sabotaged by Nazis before leaving it. (Digger)

(The Heinie plane referred to in the above photo is actually a German Messerschmitt Bf 109-4 fighter.)

John Skene, 405-F

And later we met some of the Russians along the Elb River. I recall that I didn't have very good feelings about them at the time. The first group I met turned out to be Polish, and I remember one young fellow who, for his unkempt and sorry appearance, seemed to be fairly intelligent, saying 'You better not get too excited, celebrating the finish of the war now, because some day you're going to have to fight these guys behind us'. He was talking about the Russians. He told us it had been the Russians' practice to put the Polish troops that they had in their army as point men in an attack, so that they would be the first to incur casualties from the Germans. I also recall we had some difficulties with them later, when we were moving out of what was to become their zone of occupation to our own further to the south. Don Franklin, who served as a lifeguard with two or three of us had a brother who was in the city of Erfert with a railway battalion. And I recall that became a Russian prisoner, and Don's brother was held in communicado, so to speak wasn't allowed to leave the city. He had to have an American officer come to take him out. As I remember, Don went down there to see him and found out that the Russians had told his brother that they had hardly enough food to feed their own troops -- they couldn't feed him. I also remember some Russian soldier in one town who was actually hitting Germans with the arm of a child. He looked like he might have had too much of his vodka. But the impression you got was not a very good one. This is not to say that all Russians behaved this way, because there were some who we got along with famously. They had probably suffered considerably more from the Germans than anyone else and carried a pretty big chip on their shoulders.

Greenberg 405-F
Wednesday, April 14.

As far as we were concerned our fighting days were over even though the war wasn't. We were on the banks of the Elbe River waiting for the Russians to reach us, which they did. However, before they did the 2nd armored division tried crossing the river and were thrown back. The 406th regt. sent a co. across the river, and they were all captured but were liberated two weeks later.

The Third Reich was obviously collapsing as thousands of German troops attempted to surrender to American forces rather than to the Russians. During surrender talks, German authorities had given assurance that only 20,000 German troops were in the area controlled by the Ozark Division. That number was later increased to 30,000, but in reality, over 118,000 German officers and soldiers surrendered to the 102nd Division in a one-week period.

Aerial view of the Elbe River, where the fighting ended for the 102d Infantry Division. This is the demolished railroad and highway bridge at Tangermünde where the Russians wiped out the last Nazi pocket in northern Germany.

The situation for German soldiers and civilians became desperate as the Russian troops approached the Elbe River. Germans attempted to cross the river on debris, planks, crude rafts, tire inner tubes, and in some cases washtubs. The Division history describes one German Panzer General who crossed the Elbe in an amphibious jeep with a big white flag flying. "He stood in the vehicle like an admiral on his ship's bridge and crossed the river to where a matter-of-fact soldier gave him a cold stare and asked, 'what the hell do you want?'"

The Tangermünde bridge, 4 May 1945. German troops crowd to the east bank of the Elbe and cross on the debris of the demolished bridge. A German general sailed to surrender in his amphibious volkswagen. Great stacks of arms accumulated as the Germans surrender to Ozark troops.

A page from the Division history "*With the 102nd Infantry Division through Germany*"

With the 102nd Infantry Division Through Germany:

At 6:45 PM May 4 the folks back home, sweating out V-E Day, heard Lowell Thomas say in his nightly N.B.C. broadcast: "General Eisenhower's announcement here at Supreme Allied

Headquarters tonight, seems to have put the quietus on any hope that anyone may have had for a V-E Day proclamation this week. But (his) thrilling statement, V-E Day or no V-E Day, 'German forces on the Western Front have disintegrated' -- those are his first words. 'Today what is left of two German armies surrendered to a single American division -- the 102d, commanded by Major General Frank A. Keafing.'"

On May 3, the Russians at long last appeared. To Ozark doughs of 2d Battalion, 405th Infantry (which includes F Company) fell the honor of first greeting our Allies of the east when they met, at Sandau, a war-worn but joyful party of the 1185th Infantry, 156th Russian Division. There followed many hilarious meetings and a great exchanging of compliments, weapons and decorations between these Allies, so strange and unknown to each other, yet firmly united by their singleness of purpose -- a speedy victory, then peace for all mankind.

Headquarters: Those not named are replacements. The percent of replacements in platoons were higher so you have some idea of the casualties (Digger)

John Skene, 405-F

We had crossed the Rhine River early in April, and by early May, victory in Europe day had come. We set about, in our own minds, wondering whether we would be sent to the Far East to continue the war against Japan, or remain as occupation there in Germany. Then came the point system, and all was for counting our points to see whether or not we would be eligible for return home and discharge. I recall during all of this that we were moved out of the area of Stendal, which was then becoming the Russian zone and moved to the south. At one time, I got on detached service when we set up swimming pools in some city, I can't now recall whether it was Kuelmback or Arenstock, or just where it was. But there were three of us from different parts of the battalion that managed the swimming pool.

The war in Europe officially ended at 2:41 a.m. on May 7th, 1945. The celebration in the United States was somewhat muted by the knowledge that the war continued in the Pacific.

With the 102nd Infantry Division Through Germany

The end of the war officially came for the 102nd Division at 0001 on May 9, 1945. While the rest of America celebrated, it seemed to the men of the Ozarks that the war had ended weeks before and what was uttered in Washington, London, and Paris on May 7 was something they had known for ages. Most of them wondered why it had taken so long to become official. Unlike the sudden and unexpected armistice of 1918 when orders came down to front-line troops to "cease firing," the news in 1945 was received for the most part in somber silence.

The Ozark Division understood there was still work to be done. Operation Eclipse was a directive which became effective on April 25, dictating that henceforth the 102nd Infantry Division was responsible for the security of the extensive area then under its control. This meant not only the security of the troops, but also the security of the factories, rail lines and communication networks. In some places, it also meant the administration of the German inhabitants.

Digger moved south with the 405th, to the town of Passau in Bavaria. Several of Digger's photos from this period show views of post-war Germany.

Danube River. (Digger)

(Digger)

An American Mustang that had two Heinies to his credit that was shot down and among the thousands that were being salvaged at P.W. Camp close to Passar. (Digger)

Lemondo. Some of the junk planes at P.W. Camp close to Passar. (Digger)

The General arrives. (Digger)

Airfield close to Passar. (Digger)

Group of prisoners at the P.W. camp close to Passar. (Digger)

(Authors note. Notice, even in defeat, the German prisoners are marching in step.)

This photo is of an American made Douglas A-20 medium bomber-night fighter that obviously had to land without the gear down. This aircraft has British markings. (Digger)

In June, the Ozark division was designated a Category II unit. This meant they were to perform occupational duty while awaiting shipment to the China-Burma-India Theater, or directly to Japan.

MorMor Palace (Marmorpalais), 1945. (Digger)

Gene Greenberg lists a variety of duties and duty locations that he held as part of the Army of Occupation on Germany.

Greenberg 405-F
April 19 *-- Left Gardelegen and arrived in Stendal. Guarded a Polish labor camp -- all girls.*
May 4 *-- Left Stendal for a small town called Hindenburg on the Elbe River where we celebrated V.E. day.*
May 5 *-- Collected prisoners by the thousands who came across the Elbe River.*
May 6-7 *-- The German 9th and 12th Panzer armies surrendered to the l02nd div. on the Elbe River.*
May 16 *-- Moved to Gros Moringen where we guarded V-1 and V-2 rocket bombs.*
May 29 *-- Moved 200 miles south to a town called Marlishousen. Near Erfurt.*

June 1 *-- On detail for one week guarding American soldiers who had been sentenced to death for rape and espionage. Others for life for every crime possible. Rough characters.*
June 16 *-- Moved from Marleshousen to Molsdorf.*
July 2 *-- Left Molsdorf on trucks.*
July 3 *-- Traveling.*
July 4 *-- Pitched tents near Bayrenth.*
July 5 *-- Arrived in Aigen on Czech-Austrian border.*
July 28 *-- Left on furlough to Nice*
July 30 *-- Arrived in Luxembourg for 5 days while en route to the Riviera.*
Aug 5 *-- Arrived in Nice.*
Aug 12 *-- Took plane back to outfit.*
Aug 28 *-- Moved from Aigen to Bishopgrun.*
Sept 28 *-- Went to school at Oberammergau for a week.*
Oct 16 *-- Went to Biarritz Army University for 12 weeks.*
Jan 3, 1946 *-- Returned to co.in a town called Neunburg.*
Feb 4 *-- Transferred to 406th rgt. in a town called Selb in order to go home.*
Feb 18 *-- Left for LeHavre on train.*
Feb 21 *-- Arrived in LeHavre.*
March *7 -- Leave Camp Phillip Morris on "General Anderson".*
March 16 *-- Arrive in New York.*
March 18 *-- Arrive in Ft. Dix.*
March 21 *-- Discharged.*

From the "' Up Front"' Sat. 15, Dec. 1945. (Regiment newspaper)

For a long while I've wanted to revisit a unit I traveled with in action, to see how they handled redeployment. So, I'm with Co. F. 405th Reg. again. The last time I saw them they were West of Berlin on VE day. Now they are in Bischofsgrun outside of Nurnburg. The company is down to 95 men; many having been shipped home already. Those with over 59 points have left. One of the best teams in the Division in softball is Co. F. Until redeployment they were almost unbeatable.

Riveria. (Digger)

Volk in Riviera. (Digger)

Hospital at Riveria where Harwell spent 3 months.

Jim Hansen, 405-F

The time came for us to go home. The 406th and the 407th were to go first. Those with the highest points were transferred to the 407th. The low points went to the 405th. and would stay in Germany. The 407th boarded the train at Coberg and Lichenfeld on the 17th of February 1946. After a 60-hour ride we came to Le Harve, France. We billeted at Camp Philip Morris. We loaded on the John Erickson once again. l went to the lounge and sat in a real soft chair. Quite different from the trip over.

As I sat there, I recalled, all the 102nd had seen and done. We had seen history in the making and had made some of it as well. I recalled the hard training years. The wet days in the fields of Normandy, The red ball express, the Hollanders and those nice clean bath houses. The crossing of the Roer, the push to the Rhine, and on to the Elbe. I recalled the names of the men who we lost in combat. The published reports of over 4000 enemy killed in action and of the more than 147,000 captured by the 102nd. I recalled the miseries and the ruins of a once proud people now living in squalor. There will be other wars, and America will be drawn into them but let us pick the battleground. This will not happen in America.

In closing I want to pay my respects to the men who prepared me for whatever I may have done right during the war. Life was miserable and hard during our training period. We were in excellent physical shape after the first 2 -- 3 months of training. Mentally, we were in terrible shape. Quitting was first and foremost in our minds. After many months of training, we didn't know how to quit. Now we were ready, willing, and able to do anything that was put in our path. Those that didn't reach that point suffered a terrible fate. They had reduced us to l step above an animal. The men I refer to are the cadre of the 102 Inf. Div.

With the 102d Infantry Division Through Germany

Edited by
MAJOR ALLAN H. MICK

WASHINGTON
INFANTRY JOURNAL PRESS

Digger left France aboard the S.S. Sea Scamp. One of the papers in the box of memorabilia was the final issue of the ship's newspaper, *The Sea Scamp Scoop,* dated 8 February 1946. The trip from France to the United States on this vessel took twelve days. The front-page news of the final edition contained estimates of when the ship would dock in New York.

Sea Scamp Scoop

With this issue of the Scoop we, the editorial staff, bid you goodbye. We have tried to fill the gap between the Stars and Stripes and your hometown paper and hope our effort has met with your approval. Typing stencils and drawing cartoons in a rolling, tossing ship has been no easy task, but we have done our best. Tomorrow you will find Terry and the Pirates in the N.Y. Daily News and Lil Abner in the Mirror. We've been waiting a long time.

175. SS Sea Scamp (ATC)

EPILOGUE

Digger did make it back to Senath and his family and became a well-respected businessman. So much so, that he was appointed as an Honorary Colonel on the staff of Missouri Governor John Dalton. Digger and Helen attended Governor Dalton's inauguration, and six additional invitations from the Governor's office pertain to events requiring the attendance of an Honorary Colonel.

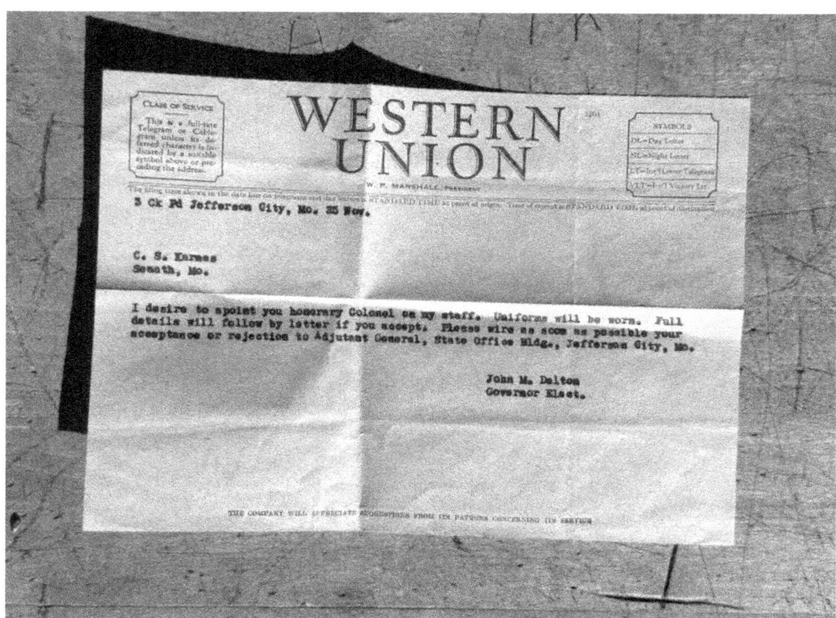

WESTERN UNION

W. P. MARSHALL, PRESIDENT

3 Ck Pd Jefferson City, Mo. 25 Nov.

C. S. Karnes
Senath, Mo.

I desire to apoint you honorary Colonel on my staff. Uniforms will be worn. Full details will follow by letter if you accept. Please wire as soon as possible your acceptance or rejection to Adjutant General, State Office Bldg., Jefferson City, Mo.

John M. Dalton
Governor Elect.

THE COMPANY WILL APPRECIATE SUGGESTIONS FROM ITS PATRONS CONCERNING ITS SERVICE

A telegram from the Governor was big news indeed!

Colonel and Mrs. Charles Sando Karnes

Digger and Helen at the Missouri Governor's inauguration Jan 9,1960.

Digger (Center) with his longtime friend Hezzie Highfill (Right), and an unidentified man, pose with a dozen pheasants. Judging from the Christmas presents in the background, the photo was taken in December, although there was no caption on the back. This photo was taken on Helen's childhood school desk from the mid-1920s, complete with inkwell, which sits proudly in our living room.

Digger, Helen, and Sue Ellen were also active in the 102nd Infantry Division Association and related annual reunions. One pamphlet in "the box" is an announcement for the 102nd Infantry Division Association's 11th annual reunion to be held at the Pick-Congress Hotel in Chicago, from July 31 to August 2, 1959. A special sticker on the announcement declares the hotel has air-conditioned rooms. It was at one of these reunions that Digger's daughter, and my mother-in law, Sue Ellen was crowned Reunion Queen, complete with a tiara.

Another bag of items in "the box" contains documents that appear to have come from Digger's wallet. These items include a Missouri driver's license that was set to expire December 16, 1966, an American Legion membership card for 1966, as well as a VFW card for the same year. Also in the bag, there was a 1965 Missouri hunting and fishing permit, a 1965 Arkansas hunting license, and a 1965 Arkansas fishing license. The final document was a Wyoming nonresident elk license for 1965, issued to Charles S. Karnes, aged 50, height 6 ft. and 200 pounds. The elk carcass tag has been removed, indicating Digger had killed an antlered elk in Wyoming.

It's the continuum of life I suppose. But that doesn't make it any less tragic. Charles Sando Karnes died at age 51 of a heart attack in Memphis Tennessee on December 19, 1965, just twenty years after the end of the War. His obituary in the Senath paper contains a list of people from out of town who attended his funeral. Included in that list are Mr. and Mrs. Edwin Harwell and son Clifford, of Oxford, Mississippi. Digger died before his time, before he had a chance to share his story with his grandchildren.

Three generations. That is about how long it takes for someone to be forgotten. After that, our entire existence is relegated to the dustbin of humanity. There is something quite sad about a family photo album containing pictures of long dead relatives who nobody can remember. Historian Stephen Ambrose once said, "the veterans of WWII did nothing less than save the world." Charles Sando Karnes was of that generation. Purple Hearts don't come free, and Bronze Star medals aren't awarded without merit. That kind of dedication deserves to be remembered. It is my hope in writing this that future generations of this family will continue to recognize Digger's sacrifices made during those dark days so long ago.

DEVOTED TO THE BEST IN

VOLUME 20 SENATH, MISSOURI FRI

Funeral Services Held Monday For Sando Karnes

Well Known Senath Business Leader

Charles Sando Karnes, one of Senath's best known citizens, passed away Sunday night, December 19, at a Memphis Hospital. A life-long resident he was known to everyone as "Digger" Karnes.

Funeral services were held Monday at the Senath Methodist Church with Rev. Glen Wiggs and Cecil Wilson officiating. Burial was in the Lulu Cemetery with the McDaniel Funeral Service in charge. Military services were conducted at the graveside by the V. F. W. and the American Legion.

Mr. Karnes was born May 17, 1914, the son of Mr. and Mrs. John M. Karnes and died at the age of 51 years.

He was educated in the Senath schools and graduated from high school in 1932. He then went into the grocery store business and since that early time has been connected with many different businesses, and also run a large farming operation.

"Digger" entered the military service in World War II in 1944. He served with the 102nd Infantry Division, known as the Ozarks. He served in both France and Germany. He was wounded in a battle at the River Elb, for which he was awarded the Purple Heart medal. He also saw service in in the Battle of the Roer, for which he was awarded the Bronze Star, and the Battle of the Rhine. He was discharged at the rank of a non-commissioned officer.

He was a member of the Barnes- Casinger - Montgomery Post 303 of Senath, a member of the V. F. W., and also served as a member of the Senath School Board a few years ago.

Survivors include his wife, Mrs. Helen Marshall Karnes, and one daughter, Mrs. Sue Ellen Hayes of Memphis, and two grandchildren, Lynn and Susan.

Pallbearers were: A. B. Utley, R. K. Swindle, Dalton Via, Alfred Moser, Dr. Charles Merryman, Lester Wilkins, Opie Clevenger ,and Marvin Layne.

Out-of-town relatives here for the funeral were: Dr. John Paul Karnes, Slippery Rock, Pa.; Mrs. John Senter Karnes, Huntsville, Mo.; Mrs. Dick Proctor, St. Louis, Mo.; Mrs. Richard P. Proctor, St. Louis, Mo.; Mr. and Mrs. Edwin Harwell and son, Clifford, Oxford, Miss.; Mrs. Scottie Rainey, Memphis, Tenn.; Mrs. Emma Greenway and son, Russell, Dell, Ark.; and Miss Margaret Marshall, St. Louis, Mo.

The following eulogy is from the funeral message by Cecil Wilson.

Matt. 17. Peter said, "Lord, is is good that we are here".

Ex.20. One of the Ten Commandments is, "And thou shal love thy neighbor as thyself".

God realizing the troubl man would have here on earth sorrow, tears and hardship. I man would only be kind, on to another life would be more bearable.

"Diggers" love for his fellow man was exceeded only by hi generosity. Befriending many many people, because of hi kindness and generosity to hi fellow man their burden wa made easier.

Indeed, it was "good for him to have been here".

This nation, and especially this city in which he lived loved and was loved, was a better place in which to live.

Many families in Scandanavi

Charles Sando Karnes obituary

Headstone and footstone: Lulu Cemetery south of Senath Missouri

POSTSCRIPT

Nearly a score of years has passed since I began this biography. During the ensuing interval, we lost Carl Schumacher, Sue Ellen's wonderful husband, which leaves a singular void in our editorial staff, and in our hearts. Digger's great grandchildren, Emily and Charles, have morphed into young adults, and the rest of us have aged gracefully, but somehow, Digger's story was incomplete. The final chapter had yet to be written.

The box of mementos which inspired this story contained Digger's Purple Heart and Bronze Star medals, and a folded American flag which draped Digger's casket when he was laid to rest with military honors in 1965. Those documents, medals, and badges are but dusty relics inconsequential to most, but they are touchstones from the past which represent a mass of experiences, many good, some unimaginable, from those dark times eight decades ago.

A burial flag holds a place of honor and respect for those serving in the military profession. I carried Digger's burial flag with me when I deployed to the desert of Southwest Asia in the summer of 2016. It was neatly folded in a yellowed plastic zip lock pouch with an American Legion sticker on the outside. That airbase in the desert was home to some of the worlds most sophisticated aircraft, which directly prosecuted America's war on terror on a daily basis. Those warplanes were a far cry from the WWII German and American aircraft pictured in Digger's photo album.

Digger's flag was aboard some of those high-tech aircraft as they flew combat missions over Iraq and Syria. Fighter aircraft are not designed to carry extraneous objects, so things such as flags are stuffed in various nooks and crannies. But a burial flag is much larger than most of the small American flags which were carried on missions whenever possible.

I first approached the operations chief for the F-22 Raptor stealth fighters, about the possibility of the flag tagging along on one of their combat missions. His initial reaction was the flag was much too large to fit in the aircraft, but something in Digger's story touched the man, and he agreed to find a place for it. On June 22, 2016, Tech Sergeant Charles Sando Karnes' burial flag was aboard an F-22 Raptor piloted by Captain Jason Reigart during a strike mission in Syria.

Folks talk on the flight line, and word spread about the big flag. When I approached the maintenance supervisor for the U-2 Dragon Lady reconnaissance aircraft, his team was prepping for the next twelve-hour mission. Their motto is, "IN GOD WE TRUST…ALL OTHERS WE MONITOR." We were sitting on the concrete floor of the hanger, leaning against the landing gear, watching the crew install the highly classified sensor package in the nose of the aircraft, when the master sergeant asked me if the flag in my lap was the burial flag he had heard about. When I said it was, he stood and carried the flag over to the crew chief and told him to find a spot in the aircraft for it. On July 9, 2016, Digger's flag flew to the edge of space, to 80,000 feet along the border of Iran and Iraq and into Syria.

An acquaintance in the Royal Australian Air Force found a spot for the flag on one of their F-18 Hornets, and on July 21, 2016, it was aboard a Hornet piloted by Squadron Leader Martin Parker, which dropped two GBU 38 laser guided bombs on an enemy position in Iraq.

The next stop was the F-15E Strike Eagle squadron, where the Ops Chief knew the story before I walked in the door and said, "we will make this happen," and Digger's burial flag was scheduled to fly on the next strike mission. On September 1, 2016, it was flown on a mission in Syria which destroyed a truck convoy.

The final stop was the EQ-4B Global Hawk squadron which flies the world's largest unmanned aerial vehicles. The crew chief later told me he realized the flag was special, so he held it until the 18th of September so it could fly on a 30-hour reconnaissance mission over Syria. A mission which was flown at 70,000 feet on the U.S. Air Force's 69th birthday.

I was initially concerned about the half century old, yellowed plastic pouch enveloping the flag, but the pouch survived five combat missions and two trips halfway around the world, and the American Legion sticker, although tattered, remains intact.

On several occasions people asked, "who was Charles Sando Karnes?" I could never adequately tell the story of a man I had never met. A man with many virtues and, like all of us, a few flaws. But the story I did tell was of a man who stepped forward, who volunteered to serve his country during one of mankind's darkest hours. A man who witnessed the vulgarities of war and combat firsthand, and returned to rural Missouri to raise a family, and who died long before anyone thought to collect the oral histories of those who survived a conflagration which claimed millions of lives.

The flag now rests in a place of honor, tucked safely in a shadow box adorned with a plate which reads -

Charles Sando Karnes - 102 Infantry Division – Germany 1944-1945

This story was written so future generations of this family will remember Digger Karnes and his sacrifices. Perhaps this endeavor will suffice as the oral history he never had an opportunity to tell.

CERTIFICATE OF AUTHENTICATION

IN HONOR OF:
TSGT CHARLES SANDO
KARNES-102 INFANTRY
DIVISION-GERMANY,
1944-1945

THIS CERTIFICATE VERIFIES THAT THIS FLAG WAS FLOWN ON A MISSION WHERE THE F-22A RAPTOR FIGHTER AIRCRAFT WAS USED IN A COMBAT STRIKE MISSION IN SYRIAN AIRSPACE UNDETECTED TARGETING AND DISRUPTING TERRORIST OPERATIONS IN SUPPORT OF OPERATION INHERENT RESOLVE

TAIL NUMBER: 04-074 DATE: 22 JUNE 2016

Captain Jason "EPIC" Reigart
90 EFS, F-22 Pilot

F-22 Raptor stealth fighter

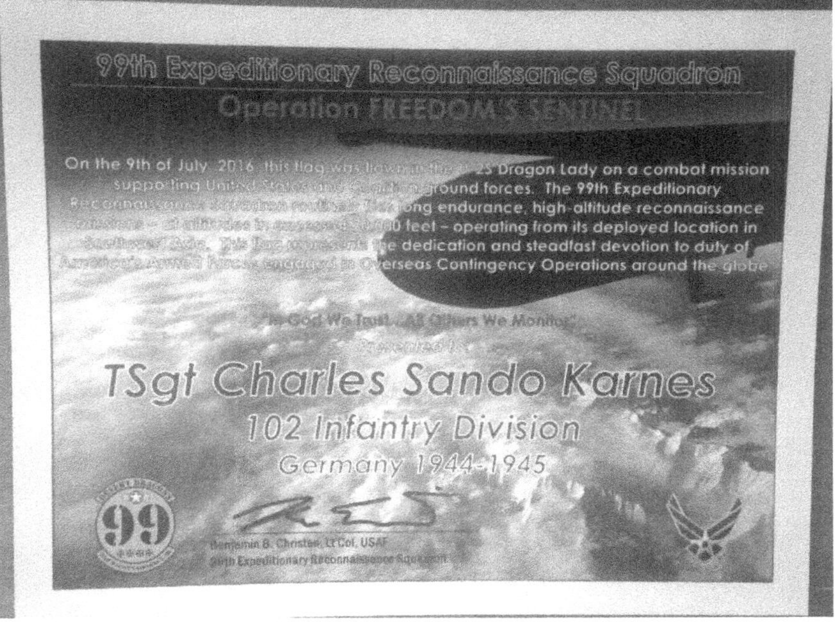

99th Expeditionary Reconnaissance Squadron
Operation FREEDOM'S SENTINEL

On the 9th of July 2016 this flag was flown in the [illegible] Dragon Lady on a combat mission supporting United States and [illegible] ground forces. The 99th Expeditionary Reconnaissance Squadron [illegible] long endurance, high-altitude reconnaissance [illegible] feet – operating from its deployed location in [illegible]. This [illegible] the dedication and steadfast devotion to duty of [illegible] engaged in Overseas Contingency Operations around the globe

"In God We Trust...All Others We Monitor"

Presented to

TSgt Charles Sando Karnes
102 Infantry Division
Germany 1944-1945

Benjamin B. Christen, Lt Col, USAF
99th Expeditionary Reconnaissance Squadron

U-2 Dragon Lady high-altitude reconnaissance aircraft

Royal Austrailian Air Force document honoring
TSgt Charles Sando Karnes

F-15 Strike Eagle fighter /bomber

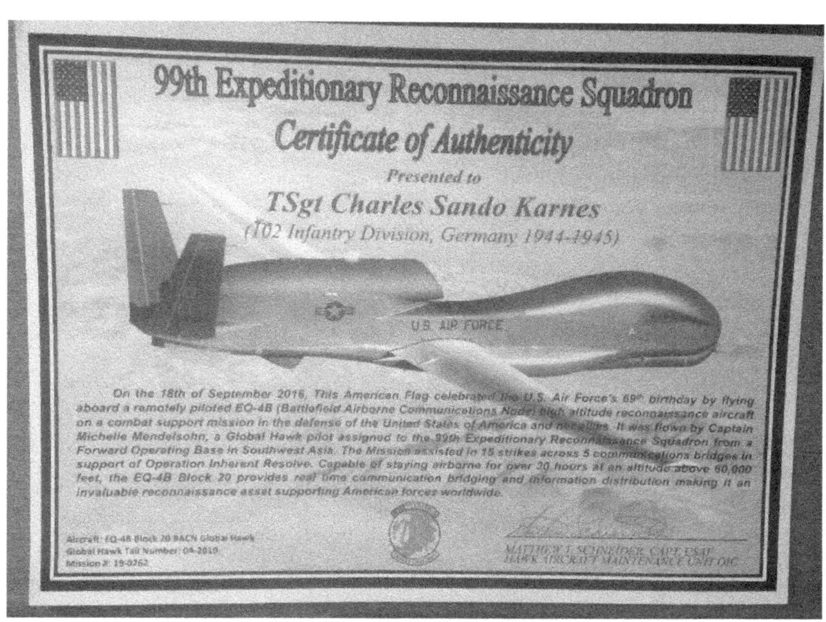

99th Expeditionary Reconnaissance Squadron

Certificate of Authenticity

Presented to

TSgt Charles Sando Karnes

(102 Infantry Division, Germany 1944-1945)

U.S. AIR FORCE

On the 18th of September 2016, This American Flag celebrated the U.S. Air Force's 69th birthday by flying aboard a remotely piloted EQ-4B (Battlefield Airborne Communications Node) high altitude reconnaissance aircraft on a combat support mission in the defense of the United States of America and her allies. It was flown by Captain Michelle Mendelsohn, a Global Hawk pilot assigned to the 99th Expeditionary Reconnaissance Squadron from a Forward Operating Base in Southwest Asia. The Mission assisted in 15 strikes across 5 communications bridges in support of Operation Inherent Resolve. Capable of staying airborne for over 30 hours at an altitude above 60,000 feet, the EQ-4B Block 20 provides real time communication bridging and information distribution making it an invaluable reconnaissance asset supporting American forces worldwide.

Aircraft: EQ-4B Block 20 BACN Global Hawk
Global Hawk Tail Number: 04-2019
Mission #: 19-0262

MATTHEW T. SCHNEIDER, CAPT, USAF
HAWK AIRCRAFT MAINTENANCE UNIT OIC

EQ-4B Global Hawk high altitude reconnaissance drone

ABOUT THE AUTHOR

Terry Creekmore is a member of the Outdoor Writers Association of America and The Western Writers of America. He has published numerous short stories in various outdoor magazines including Bugle, Arkansas Wildlife, Outdoors Unlimited, Strung Sporting Journal, Gray's Sporting Journal and Sporting Classics.

Terry grew up in the northernmost reaches of Montana before his family relocated to Northwest Arkansas in 1968. He is a retired wildlife disease biologist, and a retired Air Force Master Sergeant, and was stationed in West Germany in the mid-70s, not far south of where Digger and the 102nd entered the Third Reich during those dark days of 1944. Terry lives at the end of a dirt road west of tiny Livermore, Colorado with his wife Lynn, a blockheaded horse, and a mule named Jitterbug.

www.ingramcontent.com/pod-product-compliance
Lightning Source LLC
LaVergne TN
LVHW010929110826
845149LV00013B/2529

* 9 7 8 1 9 7 0 5 6 0 2 2 0 *